GAME PLAN

Level up your mindset.
Own your future.

DK

GAME PLAN

Level up your mindset. Own your future.

JAKE HUMPHREY + DAMIAN HUGHES

CONTENTS

FOREWORD

80 PER CENT.

That statistic is really important. Since we started interviewing the world's most incredible, successful, and well-known people, we have heard that number often.

It's the answer we were regularly given when we asked our guests how much of their success is down to the way they think. For them, just 20 per cent of their success was due to natural talent, luck, hard work, and consistency. All those things are important when discovering your own version of high performance, yet are probably only worth 20 per cent.

High performers believe the way they think – their mentality – is worth around 80 per cent. The message is clear, and the research backs this up: high-performing people are made, not born.

My name's Jake. I'm the co-host and founder of High Performance. I also co-founded one of the world's fastest-growing production companies, called Whisper Group. As well as that, I have presented kids' TV, covered Formula One, Premier League, Champions League... and much more. I would agree that in my case, more than 80 per cent of my success is down to how I think. In fact, I would say it's 100 per cent. It's that important.

When I was growing up and going to school like you, my mindset was that success was for other people, and I was destined for a life of normal, not very exciting things. Then... I read a book. I know it sounds crazy, but reading one book changed my entire life, and I hope that reading this book changes yours, too.

The book I read was called *Feel the Fear and Do It Anyway* by Susan Jeffers. It was the first time I realized that people who do great things still have doubt, still feel fear, but they still go for it. That book opened my eyes to the fact that optimism is the greatest superpower we possess. Optimism means that whatever is happening to you, you still feel hopeful for the future and that everything will be OK.

Optimism is important because it builds your resilience. You'll see the word resilience a lot in this book. It means the ability to keep going and, so often, keeping going is what eventually leads you to high performance.

There are a lot of barriers that a person can face in life. Your ethnicity, gender, socioeconomic status, disability, or neurodivergence might mean that your path to success looks different to other people's, because our societies aren't always as inclusive as they could be. While this book can't address these larger societal issues, it will help you develop an optimistic mindset that can help you overcome them.

And the greatest news of all? Optimism is available to everyone. It's something you can learn, a mindset you can build... and this book will help you build it. I wish this book had been available to me when I was your age!

And my name's Damian. I grew up in a boxing gym in Manchester, where my dad was a successful coach. I was rubbing shoulders with Olympians and boxing world champions as far back as I remember.

While their physical gifts were impressive, what I came to realize was that it was the quieter qualities that really made the difference. It was the stuff going on between their ears that helped them have the discipline to consistently show up every day, no matter how they felt; the confidence they had in themselves, even when everyone doubted them; their ability to

perform well when it mattered most. These were the qualities that I found impressive, not least because I wasn't very good at boxing, but mainly because I could use them in my own life.

Since leaving school, I have been lucky enough to work with sports teams and businesses who want to create environments where the same qualities I learned in the boxing gym can be available to everyone. I've been to three different World Cup tournaments in three different sports, written 10 books on the subject, and also taught this stuff at university in Manchester.

I love co-hosting 'The High Performance Podcast' alongside Jake, because we're able to chat to some of the highly impressive people you'll read about in this book and find out more about the quiet skills they have used to get to the top of their game, and then stay there.

You may wonder what you have in common with world-record-breaking Olympians, top footballers, business owners, and artists. What I hope you realize as you read this book is how little difference there is between you and them. When they began, they had the same doubts and fears as you may have. They also had the same dreams and ambitions as you. It is how they have chosen to deal with each obstacle and then go after their dreams that we want to share with you, so you can go after yours.

So now you know a bit about us and why we wanted to create this book for you, it's time to dive in. We hope it prompts you to ask questions, to challenge yourself, but most of all we hope it helps you realize you deserve an exciting, ambitious, adventure-filled life and helps you to work out how to find one.

Big love,

JAKE AND DAMIAN
Co-hosts, 'The High Performance Podcast'

1
INTRODUCTION

RUNNER USAIN BOLT explodes out of the starting block as if he's been fired by the very starting gun that signalled the start of his race. His head down in concentration, he pumps his arms and speeds up his stride. Within 6 seconds he is in the lead, and at 9.69 seconds he has crossed the finish line. He has become an Olympic champion and broken the 100-metres world record – and he made it look effortless.

Now, what do Usain and his powerful strides have in common with Susie Ma, founder of Tropic Skincare, as she receives an EY Entrepreneur Award for 'Building a Better Working World'? It isn't their skill sets. Those are incredibly different. It isn't their training or their achievements. But it is something that ties their skills, training, and goals together. It is their pursuit of **HIGH PERFORMANCE**.

Usain and Susie had very different career paths, and equally different talents, but they share more than we might first think. For a start, they were once young people – just like you. At one point, they decided what they wanted to do, and they decided that they wanted to do it as well as they could. Then they both found a way to achieve that goal.

That process of deciding what we want to do, and then doing it to the very best of our ability, is the essence of high performance – and do you know what? It could work for you.

You too could be as amazing as Usain and Susie, and our plan is to show you how.

OK, some of you might be rolling your eyes. What if you're not interested in being the fastest runner or creating skincare products? That's understandable, but it is also a misunderstanding.

The question is **not** whether you can become an Olympic medallist or an award-winning entrepreneur, but whether you can **think like one**.

We believe that you can, and that this new way of thinking – this **CONCEPT** of high performance – can make you the very best version of yourself, whoever you decide you want to be.

If you take pride in being fast, then – for you – understanding high performance could help you become your fastest. If you enjoy creating things, then you might just end up making a business out of it. This handbook is not about making you into someone you're not but about becoming everything you could be. We want to share how you can incorporate high performance into your own life.

We learned about high performance by looking at the approaches of people who have achieved greatness. We listened to how they formed their goals and then pursued them, and what they did when things did not go to plan.

Believe it or not, you might already have things in common with some of the greatest performers of your lifetime.

This is quite a cool thing to realize: that you share hopes and dreams with award-winning actors, or have similar doubts as double Olympians, and you might make the same mistakes as millionaires. The lessons that these high performers learned on their individual, unique journeys can be applied in your life, too, no matter what your chosen goal or challenge may be.

Our society often thinks of world champions and award-winning musicians as being talented from birth, perhaps believing that these high performers would have achieved greatness regardless of their circumstances – but it's a mistake to think this. These people might be naturally talented, but they are also products of nurture. No one was born great – they learned greatness. And, more likely than not, they learned and maintained high-performance habits.

We recently spoke to former Olympic runner Usain Bolt, a man who has arguably achieved more in track and field than almost any other athlete, and he summed up the relationship between hard work and talent better than we ever could: 'You can't get to the top with just talent alone. You need work. You need sacrifice. You have to be dedicated.'

Following on from the idea of natural talent, people often remark that high performers were 'born to do' the thing they have succeeded at. So a person might be 'born to play football', 'born to sing', or 'born to light up a stage'. But it's important to remember that they also decided to do that thing. Not only that, but they chose to do that thing really well. Indeed, they worked so hard that their high performance eventually seemed effortless. A popular saying among countless high performers goes,

THE HARDER I WORK, THE LUCKIER I SEEM TO GET. This means that the many things that appear to be luck or natural-born talent are actually the result of hard work.

It's easy to talk about 'natural talent', but it's not always obvious what a person was 'born to do'. Sometimes, our disappointments are what lead us to discover the thing that we were 'born to do'. Your teenage years and young adulthood are a time when everything seems possible, but sometimes life may not go your way and you might find yourself in a situation you never expected to be in. What sets high performers apart is how they deal with that situation. For example, take Jake Humphrey, one of the hosts of 'The High Performance Podcast'. He never planned to be a television presenter, own a production company, or start a foundation that teaches young people how to become high performers. However, he achieved all that because he failed his A levels (although we're not recommending that you fail your A levels!).

Jake might have thought he had failed on the day he collected his A-level results – but, in fact, he had just begun succeeding. He was about to make a series of decisions that would take him around the world and into a room with some of the most interesting people in the world, and it started because he failed to get into the university of his choice.

When you put it that way, it seems that a failure is only truly a failure if it doesn't start you on a new journey. Failing should really be better understood as not succeeding yet.

Jake's journey, and his choice, was to achieve high performance in a new field. He discovered that although he was not destined to be a high performer on a university English literature course, that didn't mean he couldn't be a high performer somewhere else. He had to look at where he was, think about what he could do, and then decide where he wanted to be.

Damian Hughes, Jake's co-host on 'The High Performance Podcast', followed an equally unconventional route into broadcasting. He grew up around boxers in his father's gym in Manchester, but when it became clear he would not become a great fighter himself, he realized that he could instead try to understand the people who did.

WHAT WAS THE MENTALITY THAT UNDERPINNED THEIR VICTORIES? HOW COULD MINDS BE TRAINED TO DRIVE THEIR BODIES TO GREATNESS? WHAT WERE THE PRINCIPLES THAT UNITED HIGH PERFORMERS, WHETHER THEY WERE ARTISTS, ATHLETES, OR AUTHORS?

As a result, Damian became a performance coach in a boxing gym, and worked with competitors around the world to improve their mindsets and raise their standards. Then he decided to share what he had **LEARNED**.

No one knew what podcasting was when Damian began, and few could have predicted that the lessons learned on a boxing-gym floor could change the minds of corporate CEOs, politicians, and World Cup winners. Damian simply did the best he could, where he was, with what he had (to paraphrase football coach Phil Neville), and that took him further than he could ever have imagined. Damian's life didn't go to plan, because sometimes the best-laid plans don't work out, and this can come as a surprise.

Both Jake and Damian experienced **MISFORTUNES** and made **MISTAKES**, but they soon understood the importance of controlling how they reacted to them and what they did next. Becoming a high performer is about knowing yourself and believing in yourself to the extent that you can find a way forward, even when the path you planned to take is blocked, or as yet undiscovered. High performance is about knowing that you can succeed at whatever you put your mind to.

Sounds straightforward, right? You accept that you have one life, your own unique set of skills, and a responsibility to make them count. Yes, but there will still be hardships and hurdles along the way. There will be pressure and there will be doubt, so you have to know yourself, and learn how to work through those difficult moments when emotions rise, and fear seems to pull the rug out from under your feet. You might have to learn to accept multiple disappointments and start all over again – you might even begin to enjoy these fresh starts. Whatever happens, you keep moving forward, win or lose.

Life can be **deeper**, **richer**, and more **satisfying** when you **challenge yourself.**

And you have to realize that this is the only way you would ever want it to be. You don't want to live life on easy mode, and you might grow more uncomfortable with being too comfortable, because life becomes much more interesting when you face your fears. It is worth living precisely because things don't always go to plan, and it's crucial to learn how to respond when that happens.

These are the reasons why so many of us are drawn to high performance. These are the ideas, but what about the practices? Are you ready to learn the secrets of high performance – about who you are, what your best is, and how you can make it a reality?

If you are, we'll begin. We'll come out of the starting blocks fast and we'll reach for the stars. After all, it's what Usain and Susie would do.

KEY TAKEAWAYS

1. How to identify your goals.
2. How to make the right decisions.
3. How you handle pressure.
4. What you do when you face challenges.
5. What it means to achieve your goals.
6. How to reflect on your successes and learn from your failures.

2

KNOWING YOURSELF

THE ANCIENT GREEKS believed that the centre of the world was located on the steep slopes of Mount Parnassus. They built a temple there and, over the course of many centuries, travellers came to gain the knowledge and wisdom of the gods. Philosophers and leaders arrived at its gates, falling to their knees in search of answers to the greatest questions imaginable. When they looked up, they were greeted by this inscription:

Know thyself

Like most powerful ideas, it comes in a short sentence, but its impact has lasted more than 2,000 years. If you want to understand the world, the best place to start is by understanding yourself. People have argued about the true meaning of 'Know thyself'. Is it telling us to focus on the needs of humans rather than gods, or to be aware of our own limits? And should we be thinking of our strengths or weaknesses? The truth is we cannot know the original intention of the inscription, but you can decide what you take from it. Often the most simple reading is the best one.

When you understand yourself, and the ways in which you respond to the world, you become more capable of understanding the world itself.

What does it mean to know yourself? Well, it means:

- Understanding your strengths and learning how to maximize them.
- Being conscious of your weaknesses so you can work with them, or even overcome them.
- Discovering approaches that suit you as you pursue your goals.
- Understanding the right goals for you.

You will learn through this chapter that the pursuit of **SELF-KNOWLEDGE** provides the foundation of all aspects of high performance. You have to know yourself in order to know who you want to be and to decide on the best way to become that.

It is great that you're taking time to know yourself at this moment in your life. Many people move between childhood and adulthood without ever stopping to properly think about who they are and what they want. Lots of people approach life as if it is done to them, rather than something they create through their own decisions and responses to the world around them. If you're asking yourself who you are and what you want, you're already one step closer to high performance than many of the adults that you meet every day.

Even though it is only a two-word sentence, **KNOW THYSELF** is not a simple statement. Much like 'Be kind', or 'Eat well', it is a pair of words that branches off into a series of questions that need thought and effort to answer. Knowing your strengths will be a powerful tool to help you decide on your path, but it will not be everything. You may be a fantastic mathematician and decide that, as it is your strength, you should dedicate your high-performance journey to maths. But what if your strength is not what motivates you? What if you're good at it, but it doesn't give you meaning? Maybe you hurry through your maths homework and get great marks, but find more joy spending time outside, in a park or garden perhaps. In that case, knowing yourself is about understanding both your strengths and your motivations, because a high-performance journey cannot be built on only what you're good at, but also the things that you have the drive to be better at.

So, you're going to learn about both these aspects of self-knowledge:

How to know your **strengths.**

How to find your **motivation.**

We will also help you to think about your weaknesses and how they fit into a vision of your future, and we'll teach you how to set and reset goals. Self-knowledge is a lifelong process, but asking the question 'Who am I?' is the single best place to start.

KNOW YOUR STRENGTHS AND WEAKNESSES

It is important to know what you're good at. If this is something you are also motivated to be better at, then you're finding a winning formula, but for many, this isn't always immediately clear. At school, you might know which subjects you excel at because you get good grades. This can be a helpful indicator of your strengths, but it is not the whole picture. Education is a way of providing people with a foundation for their later life, but it doesn't always test the skills that prove to be important to high performers later in life. We have spoken to many incredibly successful people, from business entrepreneur Sara Davies to rapper Aitch, who struggled at school and only really discovered their form of intelligence beyond the classroom. There wasn't a subject on the curriculum that captured what they were good at; there were no tests for Sara's skills in negotiation, or Aitch's ability to write rhymes. So try to avoid thinking of your strengths and weaknesses purely in terms of your exam results or grades.

INSTEAD, FLIP THE QUESTION FROM 'HOW CLEVER AM I?' TO: HOW AM I CLEVER?

This is a small change, but it can have a huge impact on how you think. Research on intelligence suggests that there are many ways to be intelligent, and that in all likelihood every single one of us is clever in one of those ways. This might sound like a strange idea, because our education system often creates the impression that there is only one way to be clever. People either do well academically or they do not, and that is the difference between being clever or not. We think there's more to it than that, though. Let's look at it differently.

Picture the middle-distance runner Dame Kelly Holmes and the heptathlete Dame Jessica Ennis-Hill, and ask yourself, which of them is the better athlete? If you jumped to an immediate answer, then you probably *prefer* one to the other. Maybe you're a big fan of GB athletics, or you enjoy watching running, but try to think about the question more deeply. Neither is a better athlete than the other: they are both strong and fast, and require different things from their bodies, but they were each elite in their chosen field. There are many ways to be a great athlete, with people having different body shapes and mindsets, and different approaches to speed and to endurance.

Now think about intelligence, which is something more diverse and varied than running. Intelligence combines every different way of interacting with the world and with other people. It is no surprise that there are even more ways to be intelligent than there are ways to be a great runner.

The research that led to the question 'How are you clever?' decided on eight types of intelligence, although in reality we could probably think of many, many more.

The eight types were:

Interpersonal intelligence – the ability to understand and interact with other people well, and resolve conflicts.

Intrapersonal intelligence – the ability to understand your own thoughts and feelings well.

Linguistic intelligence – good with words (written, read, or spoken). Humorous people often have high linguistic intelligence.

Physical intelligence – good at physical activities, such as sports, dancing, or building; the ability to remember things by doing rather than by reading or seeing.

Musical intelligence – the ability to think in terms of patterns, rhythms, and sounds. (If you can remember whole songs but not your PE kit, this might be you!)

Logical-numerical intelligence – the ability to problem-solve with maths or figures.

Visual intelligence – strong at visualizing things, and good with directions, map-reading, or charts.

Naturalistic intelligence – in tune with the natural world; ability to understand and see patterns in nature.

Think about which of these intelligence types applies to you. One definitely will, and maybe more. It might be that you have never felt particularly clever at school, but ask yourself how often your kind of intelligence is being tested. Maybe your type of intelligence doesn't fit with what you study at school, especially as school subjects don't necessarily test all the different forms of intelligence. Perhaps you have not yet found a way to use your intelligence to help you succeed in areas where you're less strong. Now, you might be thinking, 'I can't exactly dance my way to top marks in my biology GCSE,' and, although that is true, it doesn't mean that different forms of intelligence can't support you in getting better grades.

Maybe you often say, 'I'm not good at maths – I'm not clever.' Yet when you're out with your friends, you're the one who helps everyone come to an agreement on what you're going to do together. This means you have interpersonal intelligence. You could use your interpersonal intelligence to talk to people who do well at maths (with logical-numerical intelligence) and ask for their help on parts of the course you don't understand. Perhaps you could use your intelligence type to bring together all the people who are finding maths challenging and create a group to discuss the topics that are the most difficult. Then you could be the one to communicate this, clearly and effectively, to a teacher who could help you all.

This is an example of making your type of intelligence count. The only disappointing thing would be to never use the intelligence you have, never maximizing the many skills you offer. On the flipside, maybe you're talented at maths, but lack the linguistic or interpersonal ability that seems to make others good English students. However, you could try to make an English exam more like a maths one. Take a 30-mark essay, think about the mark scheme, and see that you get one mark for a correct answer, another for an explanation, and one more for some evidence: 1 + 1 + 1 = 3. Then you work out that 30 / 3 = 10 and you need 10 sets of answer–explanation–evidence combinations. Instead of facing a mass of words, you're now looking at a structure that fits better with your form of intelligence.

You could go even further and decide that you want to mention character, motivation, metaphors, themes, and sentence structure, or whatever your teacher directs you is on the mark scheme. You can treat them as units of information, like numbers, that you have to find and put into your 30-mark structure. You could treat your English essay more like a maths problem and play to your strengths. You will have to find the ways that suit you best, depending on the situation, but take a moment and have a think.

WHAT IS MY INTELLIGENCE?

WHAT DO I FIND DIFFICULT AT SCHOOL?

HOW COULD MY INTELLIGENCE BE APPLIED TO MY CHALLENGE?

This will be a useful way of thinking for the rest of your life, and you will also be better able to collaborate with people of different intelligence when you face a challenge. You can choose your collaborators based on the strengths they have, and how they complement and appreciate you.

Here is an exercise to help you think creatively about different ways this could work.

Think of your types of intelligence.

List a few careers that fit with these various types. (You could ask a careers guidance counsellor at school for help if you're stuck for careers ideas.)

Next, picture a friend or family member who has a different type of intelligence to you.

What could your intelligence plus theirs make?

Examples:

I have naturalistic intelligence; my sister is numerically intelligent. We could start an amazing landscaping business: I'll do the flowers and she'll do the accounts.

My mate has amazing linguistic intelligence, but I'm all about the interpersonal connections. She could be a writer, and I'll be her agent.

This is one of the amazing things about life, and about success: you can build it in whichever way you want, and you can choose to do so with people whose company you enjoy and whose skills complement yours.

Even better, as you grow, you may find that your intelligence takes you to new places and even new areas that you never thought you were cut out for. Say you have physical intelligence, but your science or numbers skills aren't as strong. Maybe you focus on sports. At some point in the future you decide you want to learn how to perform better in your chosen sport. This leads you to think about how humans build muscle. So you start to look into it and begin to understand the ideas of progressive overload (how you add weights to your workouts to grow muscles) and protein synthesis (how eating protein converts into bigger muscles). At some point in your career you realize that you started out as a sportsperson but ended up as a scientist. This is the path taken by many strength-and-conditioning coaches on professional sports teams.

Nothing is fixed and all forms of intelligence can lead to **different careers.**

We interviewed business person Jo Malone, who created one of the world's most successful perfume brands after discovering her unique intelligence. She left school at the age of 13 to become a carer for her mother, and took on work helping a local woman who made cosmetics. Eventually, Jo created a multi-million-pound business on the back of her ability to... smell. She had a nose for profit, and profited from her nose, and her story is a reminder of just how many ways there are to be clever. If you can think like Jo Malone, you may discover that your form of intelligence has great value when you take it to different places.

Similarly, you might not expect the path to financial success to start with dropping out of school. However, entrepreneur Steven Bartlett went through a similar experience. He was expelled from school aged 16 due to his low attendance, and despite his lack of interest in the curriculum, he knew he had a powerful form of interpersonal intelligence. He had a great knack for understanding people and what motivated them, and this was first proved when he was at school. One day, he overheard the heads of sixth form talking about buying a vending machine for school, and he'd interjected, saying that with 2,000 customers in students in the school, they should try and get the vending machines for free and keep the profits – which, to him, was a logical, more advantageous approach. Within a day, he made it happen. There was an element of luck that his email to a vending machine business ended up in front of that company's CEO, who, coincidentally, wanted to give back to a school. However, what was not down to luck was Steven's openness to engaging with people and his motivation to take the first step in making something happen.

Steven Bartlett also ran trips and events for the school, and was allowed to keep some of the money raised. He was so successful in this – showing that he understood what trips and events his fellow students wanted – that the school even gave him an entire wall, to advertise the things that he'd come up with. Eventually, he would be expelled because he spent more time on his businesses than in class, but those experiences were a few steps forward on his path to becoming a millionaire before the age of twenty-five, a goal that he reached two years early.

THE POWER OF LABELS

Often, other people notice our skills before we do, so it is important to listen carefully when someone tells you that you're good at something. This is often called a **GOLDEN SEED MOMENT**, when a person tells you that you have a capability that you do not yet appreciate, but you listen to them and believe them. This was the case for Olympic athletics champion Dame Kelly Holmes, whose mentor's belief in her capability changed her life. She had never thought of herself as particularly good at anything, but when her athletics coach told her that she was a great runner, everything changed. She started to think of herself as a runner, and began to behave like one.

This is a psychological effect that comes from the act of **LABELLING**. When you label yourself as good or bad at something, your behaviour changes to fit with it. If you label a behaviour positively, then you're more likely to commit to it. Former England footballer Rio Ferdinand told us how the act of telling himself that he was going to be 'a great' drove him to think and act like one. Equally, if you apply a negative label to yourself, you're much less likely to commit to improving. Avoid saying things like 'I'm bad at that', or 'I can't do that' because this will affect your motivation to improve. If you're ever tempted to use a label like that for yourself, try to reword it and say something like 'I'm struggling with that at the moment', or 'Currently I can't...' because nothing difficult is fixed forever and you can always learn new mindsets and approaches that make a difference.

Let's try a positive labelling exercise.

Positive labelling list.

Write down five things that you're good at and/or things you're proud you've done. If you're not sure, think about times when someone said you were good at something or praised something you've done.

Next to each one, write down the skills that made these achievements possible.

Keep coming back to this list, and think about how you're doing with them.

Are you improving in any of these skills?

Are you applying the same skills elsewhere?

Is there something you can do to improve a skill?

The high performers we meet often carry out this type of activity. They note down when something goes well, and also add all the behaviours and efforts they made that led to that achievement. They also scrutinize their strengths. It is not enough to just be good at something; high performance is about being the best *you can be* through mindful application. If you're good, how can you be great? And if you're struggling, how can you be better?

Now, high performance isn't all about patting yourself on the back; you have to be as conscious of your weaknesses as your strengths; but the encouraging thing is, this is all about becoming better. Tom Grennan told us that he 'likes a bit of failure' because he likes *being able* to improve.

So, on another list:

Write down your strengths in one column.

Write down your weaknesses in the other column.

Remember: these are more than just skills or talents. Your strengths and weaknesses can be repeated behaviours, mindsets you have developed, or aspects of your personality.

Could one of your strengths help one of your weaknesses?

Draw a connecting line from one of your strengths to a weakness, to think about how the strength can help to improve the weakness.

You can try this exercise for different strengths and weaknesses, and also come back to it, time and again. You might find that your strengths and weaknesses change over time.

Your strengths and your weaknesses are not separate things – they are all part of the package that make up you – so try to keep them connected in your mind. As demonstrated above, one way to look at strengths and weaknesses is to think about how your strengths can help you improve your weaknesses. However, another way is to focus on how improving your weaknesses could build on your strengths. If your weakness is failing to get up on time, but your strength is running the 400-metre race, then think about how you could run faster if you got up earlier to train. Waking up on time transforms into a new way to become faster. So try to be mindful and think about everything in terms of how it takes you towards your best, rather than trying to avoid your worst.

It will also be helpful to turn to other people who can help you understand your weaknesses, in the same way that a person could sow a golden seed moment for you by encouraging you to realize your strengths. We all find it difficult to evaluate our weaknesses because it takes a lot of **SELF-AWARENESS** to know whether or not something is being done well. In our areas of weakness, we often lack the experience and expertise to evaluate ourselves, so we are more likely to think we are better than we are. For example, 80 per cent of people think they are an above-average driver, which is impossible – only 50 per cent could be above average – but a professional Formula 1 driver would be able to tell who was good and who was not.

Dutch football manager Sarina Wiegman – who took the Lionesses to victory at Euro 2022 and 2025 – talked about the importance of accepting feedback if you want to develop your skills, and it's likely that someone will have to teach you how to improve things that are not going well. And then the more experience you get, the more confident and skilled you will become.

So look for people who have experience in the field you want to pursue, and ask for their advice. They can help to monitor your progress, outline areas for improvement, and celebrate when you progress. This kind of support can result in massive growth, as working on weaknesses often generates more progress than working on strengths. If you're scoring 90 per cent in four out of five units in an exam, but 50 per cent in the other, then you could gain a lot more marks, a lot more easily, by raising the 50 per cent than by trying to turn the 90s into perfect scores.

So now you have a sense of your strengths and weaknesses, where do you go? Where will you take them, and how far can they take you? Next, we're going to think about your goals and what motivates you.

GOALS AND MOTIVATION

Your goals will be as unique as you are: a combination of your strengths and your values, and the particular things that motivate you. As a rule, you will get your best results by committing to goals that you want to achieve, for your own reasons. Your goals should excite you, and you should feel motivated to pursue them, so first let's think about **MOTIVATION**.

Motivation is what drives us to work towards a goal. It is the thing that gets us out of bed on a cold, grey morning, and stops us from giving up when things get difficult. Many people think that rewards, such as recognition or money, keep the fire of motivation burning inside. As much as you can, try to avoid this line of thinking. The fire of motivation will be far more powerful and long-lasting if it is self-perpetuating: meaning that your motivation should come from within, and the force that keeps it alive should, too.

This is understood through the idea of **SELF-DETERMINATION**. People regularly achieve better results when their motivation comes from a sense of internal rewards, such as personal growth, rather than rewards or prizes. In tests and in life, humans repeatedly show that they are happier and more committed when their motivation for doing something comes from within. This doesn't mean that you can't also have the benefit of external rewards; it's just that they shouldn't be prioritized over your own internal ones.

So how do you build this internal sense of motivation, and how do you find meaning in doing hard things for your own sake? There are three important forces to consider.

- Autonomy
- Competence
- Relatedness

AUTONOMY

This is the ability to choose what you want to do. Think of it as the difference between being asked to clean your room because guests are coming round and choosing to do it because you want a clean space where you can revise. Research and experience on autonomy and motivation tells us that you will be more satisfied when you're cleaning for your own reasons.

Autonomy and trust are key for James Timpson, former CEO of the Timpson Group, a business that began as a shoemaker's over 150 years ago and now has over 2,000 stores offering services such as shoe repairs, key cutting and dry cleaning. He believes that trusting people to do what needs to be done is more effective than enforcing rules, which can encourage people to rebel.

Being autonomous means taking responsibility for the choices you make. Jessica Ennis-Hill talked to us about autonomous coaching relationships, where the athlete is in partnership with their coach, rather than their coach being a dictator of rules. By being in a partnership, the athlete takes ownership of their training, and quite often will win more medals because of that mindset.

Being autonomous also means having a strong locus of control. Steven Bartlett had a challenging childhood, where money was tight and both his parents had to focus on their work: 'My locus of control came from the fact that I realized very early that nobody was going to do anything for me.' Throughout his teens, Steven took the steps towards *knowing himself* and decided that he had to step away from people that he'd tried so hard to fit in with and instead embrace being true to himself, going after who he could become. To reach this kind of understanding, it's helpful to ask yourself:

WHO AM I?

WHAT DO I WANT TO DO WITH MY LIFE?

WHAT WOULD I BE HAPPY DOING IF THE EXTERNAL REWARD WAS NOT A FACTOR?

These questions can help you to seek out the sort of work that you're internally motivated by, and the answers only come by questioning yourself.

It's also important to think about the types of environments and relationships that you enjoy. You may find that you are happier when you're working in a team, or you may prefer working on your own. You may gain satisfaction from helping others, or maybe it's the act of creating something that has never existed before that makes you feel driven and motivated. Maybe you prefer short periods of really intense work (for example, you do all your weekend homework in one go), or a slow and steady approach over a longer period of time (you do one half of your homework on each day of the weekend), so think about how you work best. The key is to try different ways of working and ask yourself which one works for you. When you do, you'll discover that it never really feels like working at all. You're just being the best version of yourself. So make any project work for you, by asking:

WHAT AM I DOING?

WHEN WILL I DO IT?

HOW WILL I DO IT?

WHY AM I DOING THIS?

COMPETENCE

The second key factor in internal motivation is **COMPETENCE**. In short, this is feeling confident that you're good at something and actually being good at it, too. When you feel competent and in control, even the most challenging paths and the greatest setbacks seem like obstacles you can overcome. You know that you are the best person for the job and believe you can reach your goal.

The sense of being in control is something that we have all experienced, however small that control may have been, and we all know how much more challenging it is to endure a hardship when we feel like we are not in a position to change it. For example, when a bus is stuck in traffic, some people might prefer to get off and make their own way – even if it means, by the end of the journey, they are likely to arrive later than the bus. In such a situation, they are looking for control, so they take action to determine their own outcome.

So think about your strengths, and choose goals that can be driven by those strengths.

What can you control?

Make a list of all the things that are **outside your control** in the build-up to your exams. (For example, late buses, or even a thunderstorm on the way to the exam hall.)

Next, list the things that are **within your control**. (For example, leaving early, packing waterproof gear... and revising.)

RELATEDNESS

The third way to build internal motivation is through **RELATEDNESS**. This means feeling like you're part of a team. You can create a sense of relatedness, wherever you are and whatever you are doing.

Formula 1 racing driver Lando Norris spoke to us about spending time working with his team in the garage, even though this wasn't his job, because it allowed him to understand his individual role in the context of a related team, which only motivated him further. You too can find creative ways to build relatedness even when you are pursuing an individual goal. For example, when it comes to revision and exams, you may decide that you and your friendship group are going to get the best results possible and motivate one another. Maybe you decide that your friends from your chemistry class are going to outperform everyone's expectations. The benefit of establishing relatedness is that you can make an individual goal feel like a shared one, and see the potential for your hard work to benefit yourself and people you care about. For many of us, being part of a team is a powerful motivating factor.

However, what often motivates us the most sits in a sweet spot between our ability and our potential. When we take on a task that has the right balance between our skill (competence) and a challenge (which, through autonomy, you decide you can achieve), we often fall into a pattern of effort that has been described as a **FLOW STATE**. You may have experienced such a state yourself. In a flow state we become entirely focused on the single thing we are doing; it could be anything from solving maths problems to playing a sport or writing an essay. We may become so engaged in the task that we lose track of time, our surroundings, and any other thoughts or concerns in our life. We achieve a level of focus where nothing else in the world seems to matter.

Flow states are significant for the idea of motivation because they are incredibly effective ways to work, and are evidence that the type of work we are doing is right for us. So if you thought of something you have done when we described the feeling of a flow state, it is right for you to think of that as an area where you could achieve high performance. If you did not, let's think of some now:

What is your state of flow like?

Think of a time when you were totally focused on a task. When you did not have to 'think about thinking'; you simply acted.

Write it down and describe what you felt. (Many people describe the feeling as being like the flow of a river: their thoughts or actions connect without needing a push or a pull.)

Create a 'flow chart'.

Draw a Venn diagram with three overlapping circles. One circle represents 'Things I find challenging', another circle represents 'Tasks I enjoy', and the third circle represents 'Tasks I do well'. Make sure there is room to write in the overlapping sections.

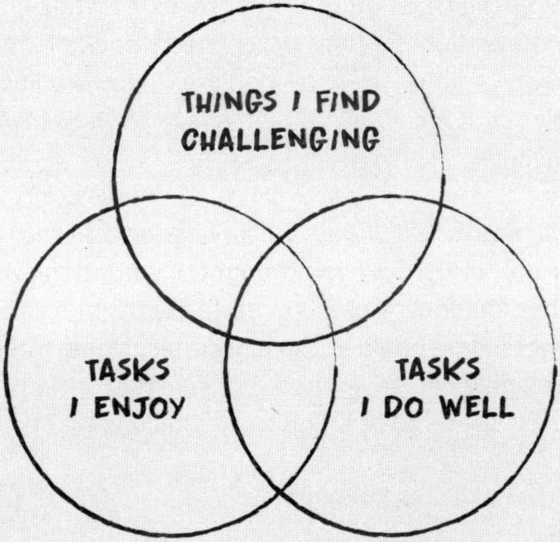

Fill each circle with tasks that are relevant to what the circle represents. Those that could fit into two or three circles should be in the parts that overlap. Those that fit into all three are activities for which you're more likely to access flow states.

The interesting thing about flow states is that the challenge is part of their appeal. Often a challenge is painted as a problem, whereas – in terms of high performance and flow – it is really a goal. You want to be challenged, and challenges can motivate us when we feel we have the skills to rise to them. In fact, many people would go as far as to argue that challenges themselves, and the flow states they enter, are the goal in their own right. This internal view of motivation reinforces the idea that it is the journey in life that motivates us, rather than the destination.

The 19th-century philosopher Friedrich Nietzsche argued that climbing a mountain for the purpose of enjoying the view from the top could never provide a route to satisfaction. He suggested that if you climb a mountain only for the sake of the achievement, you're left with nothing 'but lightning' because the moment of achievement is temporary. Former England rugby player Jonny Wilkinson echoed this when he spoke to us, remarking that his mindset when he won the Rugby World Cup only allowed him to enjoy it for about 30 seconds because he was so focused on his next challenge.

Nietzsche would argue that Jonny and all of us should focus on learning to enjoy the climb, rather than holding out for the satisfaction that comes with reaching the top or receiving a trophy. The focus on enjoying the climb rather than the destination offers us internal motivation rather than an external one based on recognition. External motivations will fade, but internal ones can take us to new and more challenging heights.

So, you have now considered the sort of goals you should pursue, and the ways in which you can pursue them.

These steps, in short, require you to:

- Know your strengths.
- Learn which strengths you enjoy using.
- Choose your goals based on your strengths.
- Label yourself as a person capable of achieving them.

- Be aware of your weaknesses and how to overcome them.
- Pick goals that are yours, that you feel competent to achieve, and that sometimes give you a state of flow.
- Remember that the best motivation comes when you love doing what you do.

So, now you've learned *what* you should do and *why*, it is time to think about how you pursue and achieve your goals.

HOW YOU REACH YOUR GOALS

Applying the principles of high performance can achieve fascinating results. Often a leader or teacher tries an 'outside the box' approach to empower or motivate others and they get surprising outcomes, which in time become principles. This notion is a high-performance principle in its own right:

There is value in approaching an old problem from a new perspective.

One example is the case of conductor, musical director, and lecturer Dr Benjamin Zander who took a unique approach to encouraging high performance. Every year he taught a group of highly capable, creative students who ranked among the most talented musicians in their national year group. He found that once these brilliant musicians entered the high-pressure environment of music college, they became so concerned about the risk of dropping marks that they lost their creative spark and stopped taking the risks that were required to go from being good musicians to great ones.

So one year Zander tried something completely different. The professor told every student in his class that they would get an A grade. Sounds great, right? All they had to do was write him a letter from the perspective of their future selves, telling him how they had got their A. Obviously a letter saying 'Dr Zander, I got an A because you gave me one' would not be enough. The students had to describe, in as much detail as possible, all the efforts they made and every step they took to get an A grade. They had to truly imagine a version of themselves that did their absolute best on the course, and look back on the previous year. The results were staggering. The students seemed to grow in focus and feel more confident in their abilities, especially in charting the path from their current state to their end goal.

The key was that the students were able to see how a top grade was possible, but equally they had visualized the real-world behaviours that could get them there. They no longer felt as though it would require some special ability or stroke of luck to achieve a top grade, but instead there was a series of steps that they themselves could picture and complete. This approach plays on the sense of autonomy that we described previously – it made the students see what was within their control – but it also worked well because it helped them to create a plan.

The power of plans is that they can connect a big goal to your current state through a series of small steps. Imagine trying to reach the top of a skyscraper with only one step; it would seem impossible and we would spend most of our time trying to devise some sort of magic rope or lift that could get us up there. Now imagine the route to the top of that skyscraper is composed of 1,000 small steps. That seems doable. When we picture our goals as huge, distant achievements, they might seem like they are one impossible step away, when in reality, they are the endpoint of a journey of 1,000 steps.

Create your own Zander letter.

Date it one year from now, and write it to yourself.

Begin with the words 'Dear [your name]'.

Then detail all the steps you took towards your goal.

It should not include any phrases such as 'I hope', 'I will', or 'I plan to'.

This is a letter from your future self, who has already achieved the goal, so it should all be in the past tense, and be absolute, such as 'I did', or 'I made'.

Include as much detail as possible: everything from the time of day you would usually wake up, to your meals and your work schedule.

Try to include some setbacks that you 'overcame'.

By the end of your Zander letter you should have a map of how you will get from where you are now to where you want to be in a year. This is the place where you have achieved your goal after following the steps that you have now thought through in advance.

BUILDING HIGH-PERFORMANCE HABITS: THE NON-NEGOTIABLES

The Zander letter uses a 'future you' to make your actions going forward seem set in stone. The 'you that has achieved them' makes the 'you that is going to achieve them' treat those actions as a part of your future because they are a part of the past of 'future you' (that's all a bit science fiction, but hopefully you get the point).

This takes us on to the idea of **NON-NEGOTIABLES**. These are the things that you want to do every time because they connect who you are with what you want to achieve.

Non-negotiables are repeated behaviours, or habits.

Almost all the high performers we have interviewed treat their habits and non-negotiables as important aspects of their success. While there can be some room for choice, or negotiation on certain things, such as your outfit or your breakfast, you need to keep in mind the habits that you repeat every time.

Non-negotiables have a number of benefits. The first benefit is that the notion of non-negotiables frees up space in your mind to focus on decisions and practice. People often spend a lot of time deciding what they should do and when they should do it, which is often not a particularly productive use of time. If you have ever spent an hour scrolling through the options on Netflix instead of just watching a film, then you have an idea of what we mean. Sometimes, choice slows us down.

More importantly, non-negotiables set our standards. This helps us to overcome motivation challenges and save us from internal debates. If you create a non-negotiable that you wake up at 7:00 am and learn to stick to it, you don't need a snooze button and you don't need to waste mental energy thinking about whether to just have a lie-in today.

The key to a non-negotiable is consistency.

Many of the high performers we have interviewed, from Olympic athlete Dame Jessica Ennis-Hill to Formula 1 racing driver Mark Webber, described a moment when they understood the power of consistency. Usually this was also a moment when they realized how much they wanted to achieve, and how important it was to use their time well. The fact is that anything great or anything hard will take a lot of time and work, and a lot of time and work never gets done in dribs and drabs. The only way to get the necessary number of repetitions completed – and the hours in – is by doing them consistently.

You cannot win a World Cup by practising sometimes. You will not create a great business by working only when you're in the mood to do so, and you will not achieve your dreams without a willingness to do certain things so often and with such regularity that they become habits, and, eventually, intuition. At the highest level, your skills need to become intuition, because any time you spend thinking about what you're doing is time that your competitor is acting on instinct.

Compare the act of kicking a ball for the first time with the 10,000th time. By the 10,000th time, it is an intuition, and the range of things you can do and be aware of will have grown massively. The very first time, you would need to think about how you are standing, how you approach the ball, and the direction you are aiming for. You could probably think about those things and manage to kick the ball in the direction you wanted to. Would you also be able to think about someone, 30 metres away, running in a different direction? Would you be able to consider kicking the ball in such a way that it would arrive at the foot of the runner, but avoid the path of someone standing in their way, trying to intercept it?

Of course not, because you would only be focused on completing the single, new behaviour, which is just kicking the ball. The person who has done it 10,000 times, however, would not have to think about how they approached the ball or making sure they managed to kick it. They have already made a habit of kicking balls and developed an intuition so they could do it without thinking. This means they have freed up their mind to think about all the other things that make kicking a ball really effective. They have built up their base of foundational, repeatable skills, so they can concentrate on more difficult aspects.

This is a key component of high performance. You need habits to form core skills that allow you to apply them in increasingly complex ways, in more difficult situations. You need to be fast, accurate, and capable of multitasking, and you can only focus on speed, accuracy, and multiple tasks if you can complete the basic tasks without thinking. This is something the iconic rugby coach Ian McGeechan calls 'world-class basics'.

Take the example of a great chef: we may think it is all about serving nutritious meals and creating delicious recipes, when really it is about cutting lots of onions. Huh? Only by cutting thousands of vegetables will you be able to do it efficiently and fast enough to focus on all the complex aspects of serving a meal to 100 people in a restaurant. You can't do the great thing unless you can do the small things without even thinking about them. To look like you were 'born to do' something, you need world-class basics.

The other key aspect of repeated behaviours is that they allow us to perform under pressure. Imagine trying to kick that ball – for the very first time – but someone tells you there is £1,000,000 on the line if you score, and a fine of £1,000 if you don't. Now you're doing something difficult, and new, under pressure. You can guarantee that you would wish you could have practised the kick a few times before the one that counts.

For runner Keely Hodgkinson, at the 2020 Tokyo Olympics, the benefit of this repetition meant that she didn't let the pressure overwhelm her. She'd already run many 800 metres, and in Tokyo she had the mindset of it being **JUST ANOTHER RACE, IN A REALLY BIG STADIUM**.

All our high performers learned to make hard things feel easy, so that when pressure was introduced, they could rely on their core skills and use their brains to manage the pressure and be creative. This is why consistency in practice, delivered through non-negotiables, is vital.

TRADEMARK BEHAVIOURS

Some of these high performers prefer to define their non-negotiables as **TRADEMARK BEHAVIOURS**. We have talked previously about how effective it is to give ourselves positive labels, like 'I'm a good runner', but trademark behaviours give you a way to label your behaviours as well. Maybe you create the label 'I work hard', then the trademark behaviours 'I wake up early', 'I revise until lunch', 'I go to the gym', and 'I work until dinner' can all follow on from this.

There is no debate to be had about these things. They are the next step from a positive idea you have about yourself, and they get done. Of course there will be times for rest, when you go on holiday, or after you've completed your goal, but while you're pursuing it, your trademark behaviours will be your best friend.

Trademark behaviours can be **small things.**

Maybe you decide that your desk is always clean, or that you always have fruit or vegetables with every meal. Olympic cyclist Dame Laura Kenny told us that one of her trademark behaviours is that she always arrives 10 minutes early for things, and another is that she shows respect to everyone, no matter what they do. What is important is that you decide who you want to be, and which trademark behaviours make up that high-performing version of yourself, no matter how small they may seem.

Research into high-performing businesses shows that they often motivate and reward staff for applying small trademark behaviours, such as arriving at work on time, rather than the outcomes that they may achieve. Results are much better when the incentive is to do the small things right every time, rather than rewarding people when an overall outcome is good. Sometimes outcomes involve an element of luck, whereas trademark behaviours are something you can control every time.

Trademark behaviours.

Think about the positive labels you have for yourself.

What are the **trademark behaviours** you want to associate with these labels?

These trademark behaviours will provide you with core skills that you can rely on when the pressure is on, such as when the exam starts, or the referee blows the whistle. You may also find it helps to develop some of these habits into **RITUALS**, which can make you feel calm and prepared when the moment to perform arrives. Usain Bolt told us how his famous crowd engagement before races was a part of his ritual that gave him confidence, while footballer Scott McTominay takes a moment to stop and smile before big games because it reminds him to be grateful for his job as a professional footballer.

The Rugby World Cup-winning coach Sir Clive Woodward created a simple ritual for his team, which they would go through at half-time in every game. The first two minutes of half-time were spent in silence, thinking about the team performance in the first half and putting on a new kit. The next three minutes required players to listen to Clive's assessment, and at the same time, take on food and fluids. They would then listen to the captain's last words before spending the final two minutes in silence again, visualizing the start of the second half. This meant that no matter how challenging the first half had been, they had something they understood and felt comfortable doing at the end of it. They would also then step out for the second half of each game in exactly the same frame of mind that they did for every other game, which was particularly useful when the pressure was on.

Let's try to create a ritual for you, and apply it to the classic high-pressure environment of an exam.

What is your exam ritual?

List a set of behaviours that you will do every time you have a test (beyond revision, of course!). This set of behaviours will become your ritual.

The behaviours might include your wake-up time, your choice of breakfast, and the way you enter the exam hall.

Practise these behaviours on regular school days. For example, enter a classroom in the way that you might enter the exam hall.

This helps you feel in control, sets your standards, and reminds you that an exam is simply another routine.

It follows a process, and it is something you have done many times before.

This is just another way of knowing yourself, and of using routine to create a version of yourself that is comfortable performing at a high level and under pressure. If you know what you're capable of, and have habits that you believe in, there will be no need to doubt yourself. What starts with self-knowledge becomes a series of behaviours that you can rely on, every time. So, try to think positively about yourself, know you're in control, and exercise that control consistently. It is the best way to get results.

KEY TAKEAWAYS

1. Know yourself. How are you clever?
2. Improve on your weaknesses. This can be as powerful as maximizing your strengths.
3. Choose goals that motivate you. Ones that apply to you and that make you feel capable.
4. Set your goal and think about the steps that will take you there. What are the small things you need to achieve to get you to your goal?
5. Create trademark behaviours and rituals to maintain consistency, in order to take the steps towards your goal.

3

MAKING CHOICES

IN MANY WAYS, our life is the sum of our choices. We are born with talents and experience events, but our choices are the one thing that we are truly responsible for. Yet people often fail to actively think about their choices and how or why they should make them. People often make choices because of the way they've been taught, which is the way things have always been done, or they make choices on the basis of what their friends are doing, or what their parents would want. The reality, though, is that your sense of control, motivation, and likelihood of success will all be driven by the extent to which you own, or take responsibility for, your choices – and make them based on an understanding of yourself and your goals.

So, you should think about choices, big and small, with the self-knowledge developed from spending time getting to know yourself, and you should do so with an attention to detail that would make a high performer proud.

Many of the high performers we've interviewed pay attention to even the smallest choices. They realized, from a life of competition, that:

Small choices can add up to make **big changes.**

Formula 1 team principal Toto Wolff told us how he turned around the Mercedes F1 team when he took over, and his answer surprised us. He reeled off a list of seemingly minor changes he had to make, focusing on things like cleanliness and order in the offices, rather than the big sweeping changes you would expect to make at a multi-billion-pound engineering company. Toto saw that the big problems were best approached by implementing small changes. In his eyes the larger adjustments, such as updating the car and driver training programmes, would be better achieved once they had got everything working behind the scenes. Seven consecutive world championships later, it seemed he was right.

Toto Wolff not only understood that the foundation of major change is often in small choices, but he also demonstrated his ability to think flexibly. We have discussed flexible-thinking approaches, such as approaching an English question mathematically or becoming a scientist through a love of sport, and these problem-solving approaches are applied by high performers every day. They find ways to do things differently, because often it is only by doing things differently that you can do them better.

Pick a big goal that you have.

Now make a list of the small choices that might make a difference while you pursue it.

CHANGING PLANS AND THINKING FLEXIBLY

Imagine that at the end of this year all your plans fall apart. Maybe you don't get the grades you want, or events dictate that you cannot take your next step in the direction you were expecting to. What could a total reset in your plans look like? This may be scary to think about now, but you have to practise thinking flexibly, because when the time comes and such thinking is required, you will be better prepared. So think about your skills:

WHAT TYPE OF INTELLIGENCE COULD I DRAW ON IF I HAD TO SWITCH TO PLAN B?

WHAT NEW HURDLES MIGHT I FACE AND WHAT OPPORTUNITIES MIGHT COME MY WAY?

HOW MIGHT I NEED TO THINK DIFFERENTLY?

Maybe you planned to study law at university, but your history A-level result wasn't what you needed for the course. Step one of flexible thinking might be to consider spending another year studying and retaking the exam. This would not be the end of the world; if you are set on becoming a lawyer and that is your goal, then a one-year setback is something you can overcome. Maybe you decide to start on a completely new path; you think about ways in which you're intelligent and decide to become a baker, a singer, or a salesperson instead. You have thought about pursuits that give you meaning, and areas where you have experienced flow, and decide on a suitable new path for yourself. You may not go to law school, but you might realize that it was the best thing that ever happened to you.

By being aware of your strengths and conscious of how good habits, such as consistency and flexible thinking, can make you a high performer in any field, you can **PIVOT** from one goal to another and see the new opportunities that come with it. We've seen it time and again: we've met former civil servant Chrissie Wellington OBE, who pivoted to become four-time World Ironman Champion; soldier Aldo Kane, who became a television presenter; and Muhammad Ali's daughter Laila Ali who – at the age of 18 – pivoted from owning a nail salon and not doing any sports to becoming a world champion boxer. All these examples remind us that it is never too late to make a change, and it certainly isn't too late if you are in your teens or twenties.

When we think about our skills, it is important not to be too focused on natural abilities. If we build on self-identifications, such as 'I am fast', or 'I am good at public speaking', then we are less free to pivot than we would be with labels like 'I work hard,' or 'I take time to listen to people'. These effort-based skills are more flexible and transferable than those based on natural ability, so they have the potential to work for you in any field you choose.

REMOVING CHOICE

One of the best ways to improve our decision-making is to remove choice. In the same way that non-negotiables can free up our mind to focus on negotiables, turning small choices into action frees us to do more, and to think more about the things that matter.

An action trigger, or an **IMPLEMENTATION INTENTION**, is a simple approach that means you commit to doing something *because* you have done something else. This can allow you to create a chain of positive actions that draw less on your reserves of motivation because they simply follow on from one another. So, for example, if you struggle to fit organization into your schedule, you could create the action trigger 'When I finish revising, I will clear my desk.' This takes something you will have to do, and tacks on something you might otherwise not. It turns clearing your desk into something you don't have to think about because you have made a choice to *remove the choice*.

Creating action triggers has been found to be a very effective way to establish consistent positive behaviours; it saves an amount of planning time and a number of self-imposed pep talks. Say, for example, you struggle to plan out your revision days, or find that there are parts of the day when you lose focus or motivation. Action triggers could set you on a more effective path. They could go something like this:

WHEN I WAKE UP, I WILL BRUSH MY TEETH.
WHILE I BRUSH MY TEETH, I WILL LOOK AT MY REVISION CARDS ON THE BATHROOM WALL.
AFTER I LOOK AT THEM, I WILL EAT BREAKFAST.
WHEN I FINISH BREAKFAST, I WILL LAY OUT MY REVISION MATERIALS.
AFTER I LAY OUT MY MATERIALS, I WILL READ THROUGH MY TEXTBOOK.
WHILE I READ THROUGH MY TEXTBOOK, I WILL MAKE NOTES.
AFTER I FINISH MY NOTES, I WILL HAVE LUNCH.
AFTER LUNCH, I WILL TURN MY NOTES INTO REVISION CARDS.

And so on...

What starts as the simple act of waking up and brushing your teeth turns into a repeated pattern of effective work, which feeds into your next day as you have created the revision cards that will start your next morning.

Create your own daily routine based on action triggers.

Follow the previous example to create your own action triggers.

Often these triggers become habits and take on their own momentum. They build into one another until you have a whole timeline of positive behaviours leading to your goal. They also save you from making small mistakes that can, unchecked, become big problems. Your action triggers can include all aspects of your preparation, and that might mean you remember to do something that could have been a problem if forgotten.

The great basketball coach John Wooden captured this idea well by insisting on routine tasks, all the way down to how his players put on their socks before a game, because he realized this could make a big difference.

'Socks?' you might say. Well, hear him out.

He told his players to put on their socks carefully, to make them fit their feet and iron out any wrinkles. Avoiding wrinkles meant fewer blisters. Fewer blisters meant less time off the court getting a plaster or changing socks. And time off the court might mean you were not in place to make a block. That block might be the difference between winning and losing a championship. From socks to blocks to national championships, John saw how small things could have a knock-on effect. Just like Formula 1's Toto Wolff, John realized that big achievements are built on foundations of small decisions, so it made sense to do those small things well.

The other reason you might decide to focus on making small choices comes from the idea of **MARGINAL GAINS**. This idea was popularized by the British Team Sky cycling team and it is a simple one. When you bring together high performers to compete against one another, they will all be broadly doing the big things correctly. The annual multi-stage bicycle race known as the Tour de France will have teams of gifted cyclists who work very hard and ride the very best bicycles. But it is doing the small things slightly better than their opponents that will give a team an advantage. A better pillow might give their cyclists 10 per cent better sleep than their rivals, which might result in a one-second advantage on the course. One second can be the difference between first place and fourth place. For Team Sky, they realized that not only were the big things built from the small things, but that the small things could often make the difference between winning or not.

Marginal gains are most relevant when you have already ensured that you're doing all the obvious things correctly. You're setting goals, living healthily, and working hard. These aspects of high performance are key to your non-negotiables because they are the essence of every high performer's routine. Every great person you have ever seen worked incredibly hard to get to where they are. No debate. They may have been naturally gifted, but in a world of billions of people, there will always be someone of similar or greater talent. At that point, it is only the hard work or the quality of preparation that will separate you from the others.

BIG CHOICES – WHO YOU WANT TO BE

If you commit to working hard and to maximizing your potential, you will have to make a choice that this is who you are. We have discussed knowing ourselves, but we can also choose ourselves. This is the definition of a **BIG CHOICE**. You can change your sense of who you are.

Identity change is a key driver of **habit change.**

So the first step is to think of yourself as a high performer, as it will be essential if you are to act like one. This is a positive label that can lead to many more **POSITIVE** decisions.

This was something that former footballer Rio Ferdinand spoke to us about on the podcast. He was incredibly talented and flew through the youth ranks, but struggled to make the leap from young talent to future great. By his early twenties he had reached the Premier League, but his progress had stopped. He was enjoying his life as a successful young footballer, taking it easy at training and partying at night, but the outcome was that he underperformed. Rio was left out of the England Euro 2000 squad, and it proved to be a wake-up call. He couldn't just look at himself as a footballer, or even a Premier League one, because he wanted to be elite, so he had to think of himself in that way. Once he decided that he was a champion he behaved like one, and that helped him become one.

Of course, for Rio, this took a great deal of self-belief and a willingness to own his identity. He had to accept that some people might not appreciate his more focused lifestyle, but it was necessary for his success. Fortunately, he already had experience of refusing the limitations his peer group put on him. As a teenager he took ballet lessons, which developed his co-ordination and core strength, but also gave him the strength of character to continue even when his friends mocked him for it. He chose his high performance over the validation of his peer group and took ownership of his **IDENTITY**.

This idea of a **CHANGE** in our identity driving us to new and better behaviour is well researched. Many of us believe people make decisions based on the consequences they expect, but in fact, studies have shown that people often make decisions based on who they think they are. If you identify as one sort of person, you're likely to make decisions that such a person would make, even if those decisions are not necessarily in your self-interest. A rich person who thinks of themselves as 'a caring person' will vote for tax rises that cost them more money but will benefit others. Similarly, a self-labelled 'environmentalist' is more likely to take a train than a plane because they have given themselves a name.

So call yourself a high performer, a hard worker, or even start thinking of yourself as a trainee in whichever field you want to pursue. Maybe you want to be a doctor, so call yourself a future doctor or say you're training to be one. Even if you're not studying medicine yet, you are still in training.

- ▶ Label yourself and make the choice to act like a high performer.

- ▶ Choose the habits that will lead to high performance and choose to be consistent.

- ▶ This is the best way to become who you want to be, and perform when the pressure is on.

It is also important to develop a sense of identity because there will be times when other people try to distract you from your path. The people around you and the culture that you live in may not appreciate the choices and sacrifices you're making. If you have ambitions and your friends don't, be prepared to do things differently from them. Lean on the identity you have created for yourself and accept that you will have to stand out from the group at times.

All high performers have to accept this, and some even relish the fact that they developed a professional identity above and beyond what their friends expected of them. Social-media influencer 'JJ' Olatunji spoke to us about how the identity he created for himself as KSI allowed him to be an extrovert when, in reality, he could be quite the opposite in his personal life. Similarly, British rapper Aitch distinguished between his professional identity as a rapper (Aitch) and as a man (Harrison Armstrong), and the fact that his professional identity allowed him to receive criticism (which as someone in the public eye he expects), and treat it as an aspect of his job. Harrison created the professional identity of a performer, and it allowed him to accept negative feedback as a response to his performance rather than himself.

Both Aitch and KSI had to accept that if they were going to be high performers, they would have to stand out from the crowd – and you too may have to face the prospect of not fitting in if you have goals that you're pursuing. You may choose to work when your friends want to relax, or you may prioritize training in the morning instead of going out late. You have to show strength of character to make those choices, because other people will often want you to live like they do. Dame Laura Kenny told us that she had the mindset of 'I need to do everything that's right for my performance', so she missed parties and didn't really celebrate her 21st birthday because her ultimate goal was to win gold medals.

However, making a choice to commit to your goals doesn't have to mean losing friends. Television star and author Vicky Pattison advocates for surrounding yourself with 'positive pigeons' – or 'igniters' – people who inspire you and **SUPPORT** you.

Many other high performers, particularly sportspeople, have had to accept certain sacrifices in the name of their goal, but if you have labelled yourself as a particular, high-performing type of person, this sacrifice will only feel easier. So own it – and remember that you can and will find others who **ACCEPT** and support your choices.

OWN YOUR CHOICES

Owning choices is a recurring theme in the life of a high performer. This is because taking responsibility for your decisions, whether they were the right or wrong ones, is very important for developing a sense of responsibility for your own progress. Essentially this means being aware of what you can control, and accepting that certain aspects of our lives are beyond our control.

After you develop this awareness, you can focus on:

- Controlling the controllables.
- Deciding on those things that you can improve and dedicating your energy to them.

This does not mean ignoring any misfortune that might come your way. You should still be able to recognize when difficult or unfortunate things occur, but you have to be aware that when these things happen, you don't have any power to change them. Energy spent thinking about how unlucky you were is energy you could have spent responding to the problem that you faced.

Your response is the only thing you can really control in the face of misfortune.

The high performers we have met can quickly separate the things that have happened to them, which are beyond their control, from their responses, which are in their hands. For Dame Jessica Ennis-Hill, she talked about how one heptathlon event might not have gone well, but she had to be able to switch her focus to the next event: 'I can't change anything that I've done, but I can change the next few steps and the way I approach the next event, the next championships, the next training session...' This mindset is very powerful, because the more in control of your life you feel, the better you will do.

High performers will experience moments of success, because that's what they've been working towards. Many of our guests, including Dame Jessica Ennis-Hill, emphasized the importance of enjoying those moments, but not at the expense of others. Laila Ali recounted that her father had always told her and her siblings to 'never step on others to get ahead', or, as she put it: 'don't dim someone else's light to make yours shine'.

We discussed this in the chapter on knowing ourselves, but it is worth repeating. Our sense of responsibility and control can impact our academic results, our motivation, and even the length of our lives. Taking responsibility for your responses can even protect you against mental health challenges such as stress and depression, but you have to develop the mindset to feel in control. So, when you find yourself focusing on some bad luck or a problem that seems to have been put upon you, try to think about it as just that: bad luck, which is out of your control. Then try to think about the aspects of your response you will be able to control, because these are the moments when you develop the mental strength that will support you through your whole life.

Unfortunately, many of us focus too much on things beyond our control every day. Sometimes this becomes habitual, and defines so much of a person's experience of the world that they spend much of their life in a state of constant anxiety. This anxiety is a serious mental health condition, but for many people who are not suffering it to the extent where they need professional support, there are techniques, practices, and resources that can help improve the experience of low-level anxiety.

MANAGING ANXIETY

Anxiety is often connected to a feeling of being out of control, when you worry about events that may happen, reactions people might have, or things you could do wrong. If you're experiencing anxiety, but feel you can manage it yourself, the practices around making choices could benefit you.

In this section it is important to note that we are not providing professional mental health advice or counselling. If you have a more serious anxiety condition, do seek professional help.

If you struggle with anxious thoughts, try to remind yourself of the importance of controlling the controllables. Ask yourself whether the thing you're worrying about is something you can control. In many cases it will not be, and in such situations, it is worth focusing on the things you can control.

You may suffer from climate anxiety, worrying about the state of the planet and the future of human civilization. This is a legitimate concern, but not one you can control on an individual level – the problem exists on a much bigger scale than you can manage. So the best option is to focus on the solutions you can influence. Taking action will not only make you feel better, but the restless energy that is being spent on anxious mental loops will have an outlet for release.

Many of us develop anxiety about things that are beyond our control, but there is always a way to regain a sense of ownership of your thoughts and feelings. In these cases, the controllables may not relate to the subject of your anxiety as much as the way in which you're thinking and behaving.

For example, maybe you have a constant sense of dread about the safety of people you care about; you often find yourself worrying that a loved one is safe. In these situations, it is important to treat the part of you that is engaging in patterns of anxious thought as only one part of your brain – and that less rational part is in control – then you have to acknowledge that you are engaging in a pattern of anxious thought. Maybe it is helpful to label that part of your mind and treat it almost like a friend that has a tendency to worry. Take it on yourself to reassure the anxious part of your mind, and ask questions, such as:

DO I HAVE ANY REASON TO BELIEVE THIS?

IN MY EXPERIENCE, IS THIS SOMETHING THAT OFTEN HAPPENS?

If you take the time to question your anxiety, you're more likely to reach a more comfortable conclusion: that your anxious mind is not your whole mind, and that the anxiety-driven part is not giving you an accurate account of your situation. Psychologist Dr Pippa Grange described this as 'see, face, and replace' – the process of engaging with your fear rather than trying to escape it, by questioning it and then reshaping it into something that you can manage.

There is another form of anxiety that is less focused but just as troubling: the anxiety about nothing in particular. This experience of anxiety is a way of thinking that can be applied to any and every aspect of our lives. To improve your experience of this kind of anxiety, you can apply the techniques mentioned above, such as reminding yourself to control the controllables, or questioning the logic of your anxious thought, but it is more likely that this pattern of behaviour will need consistent approaches.

The first approach is: **talk** about what you are **feeling**.

This is a great way to make anxiety a less lonely experience, but it is also helpful because it gives you access to another perspective. Just as we have discussed the positive impact of finding strength in our 'relatedness', and gaining motivation from the belief that our mentors or coaches have in us, so too can other people help us engage with our fears, doubts, and anxiety.

Television personality Jamie Laing told us about how his therapist's perspective, and their careful questioning, allowed him to become wiser about himself, and to differentiate between negative and positive thoughts and behaviours. Similarly, Dame Jessica Ennis-Hill told us how, during the 2012 Olympic Games, she and her team regularly sat with a sports psychologist, both individually and as a team. The athletes understood that it was important for them to communicate how they were feeling, and to listen to how others were interpreting the pressure of the situation. You may prefer to talk to one of your friends, or to an older person you respect, but the key fact will be deciding who you trust and whose advice you value.

Talking is particularly important when you feel anxious about your choices. You're at a point in your life when there are a number of choices to make, and it is easy to feel overwhelmed. This is normal, and although we believe in knowing ourselves and making choices based on the way we see ourselves, it is always helpful to access another person's perspective. So think of someone who knows you, but also possibly someone who might think differently to you. They may make an observation about your life path or suggest choices that sound surprising, but take the time to listen. Consider what they tell you. Ask them how they think their suggestions might work for you; they may be able to see your skills from a new perspective.

Another option for dealing with general anxiety is to consider this:

Exercise can benefit your mental wellbeing.

The overactivity in our minds that occurs with anxiety often feels more balanced and manageable when there is physical activity to go with it. You can put this to the test even when you're not facing anxiety but have a difficult choice to make. Go for a walk and see how differently your mind works when you're in motion. Remember that the anxious part of our brain has been in place for thousands of years, and was designed to deal with threats, and the best way to resolve threats as an ancient human was by the fight-or-flight response – to either stay and fight the problem or escape it altogether.

In most cases, your choices cannot be made by fighting or moving, but the part of the brain that evaluates them can be less consumed by worry if it feels that you have taken some physical action. A walk can be enough, but intense physical exercise will often have an even greater impact. We spoke about how flow states work, and how they can generate very productive outcomes, and the same can be said for the flow states that you achieve through intense exercise. These flow states can leave us with a sense of mental clarity that allows us to look at our problems, or the subjects of our anxiety, with calm, rational focus.

So next time you have a big choice to make, don't sleep on it, but run on it, lift it, throw it, and catch it, until you have calmed your mind by working your body.

Once you have finished your workout, you may find that you're in the right headspace to consider your choice, and at this point it is great to engage in some research.

Research is another way to **re-establish control** in the face of **doubt.**

Researching a situation that you're facing can help you manage the fear that can grow when you don't yet understand the reality of a choice or problem.

Are you feeling unsure about your choice of university? Research the university: everything from the quality of the course to places to hang out, groups you can join, and the nightlife to experience. Whether you end up impressed or unimpressed, you will feel informed, and often anxiety is built on a lack of information, uncertainty, or doubt. Knowing the pros and cons of a choice allows you to reassert your control, and believe in your own reasons for making it.

Finally, you may find yourself suffering from anxiety in the run-up to stressful or high-pressure events, such as exams. This is normal, and is a reflection of the importance of the task you're undertaking and the opportunity you have to do well. This form of anxiety is a response to pressure, and there is a chapter dealing with pressure coming up. The important thing to remember is:

Pressure is **normal**. It's a logical response to doing something **challenging** and **pursuing an opportunity** that you really want.

Another way to think about pressure is that it's a privilege. If you're in a position to experience pressure, you're stretching yourself and facing a challenge. The reason you don't feel any pressure sitting on the sofa is because there isn't an opportunity in that situation, so learn to appreciate it and then learn to control it.

Remember you are in control. You're gaining greater control over your life every day, and this is a positive thing.

Control means **independence**.

It is an opportunity to use our skills and be our best; it means making choices and living by them. A life is the sum total of a person's choices. You were born with talents, and you experience events, but it is up to you to choose your responses to them. This is what it means to be alive; this is what it means to be free.

KEY TAKEAWAYS

1. Appreciate that you have the freedom to make choices in your life.

2. Sometimes small choices are at the heart of big achievements. What are the small things that you can choose to do every day that will help you reach your goals?

3. Think flexibly. Be prepared to make a choice that you were not planning to make, one that you come to after approaching your challenge from a new direction.

4. Use action triggers: if I do X, then I will do Y.

5. Give yourself positive labels. Make the choices that such a person would make.

6. Take ownership of your choices, and your life. You get to choose and you get to be responsible for what happens in your life.

7. Manage choice anxiety by taking action – by talking, by researching the options available to you, and by exercising.

4

HANDLING PRESSURE

PRESSURE IS THE space between the weight of an opportunity and the rising fear of missing it. It is a feeling that you experience when you know there is something to aim for, and that goal requires you to do your best. The key is to remember that you're far more likely to deliver your best when you remain calm and focused, and to treat the pressure as a necessary and manageable feature of high performance.

Rugby World Cup winner Dan Carter told us that he sees pressure as a privilege. You only really get to experience it when there is something on the line, when you're testing or stretching yourself. You have to learn to appreciate the pressure, because it is a sign that you're working in a space where things *really matter*. Think about footballers: they experience pressure in cup finals but not friendlies. Actors and musicians work under pressure when there is a full audience, but less so in dress rehearsals or on nights where hardly any tickets have been sold. You might face pressure in an interview, especially if it's something you really want – perhaps a job, a university place, or even a financial loan. Pressure is, in many ways, the thing you want. If you care about what you're doing, then you won't be satisfied with only friendlies or interviews that don't matter.

You practise to be ready for the real thing, and the real thing means some degree of pressure.

MANAGING YOUR EMOTIONS

So you should accept pressure and learn to manage it, and that means managing your emotions. If you don't, your emotions will manage you. We've interviewed numerous high performers, and in particular athletes, who have stories about moments when they let their emotions overcome them and failed to execute their plans as a result.

Olympic cycling champion Sir Chris Hoy, who won six gold medals, told us about the time when he watched his rival break the world record in the lap before he was due to race. Chris knew that he could beat that time; he had the practice and the evidence to tell him that he could do it if he stuck to his plan, but the pressure and his emotions took him off-script. He panicked; he abandoned his strategy and tried to race at full throttle from the first second of his race. As a result, he tired himself out long before the finish and failed not only to match his rival, but even to post a time he could feel proud of.

Olympic athletics champion Dame Kelly Holmes had a similar experience. She let pressure dictate her decisions in a world final and raced on emotion, rather than planning, and got the same result as Sir Chris Hoy. They are both high performers; they had experienced pressure before and they would experience it many times after, but they learned valuable lessons on those days. You have to control your reaction to pressure and the adrenaline it creates, because while adrenaline can drive you to be better, too much of it will ruin your performance.

FOCUS ON WHAT YOU KNOW

You want to be motivated by pressure but not overwhelmed. This is why it is important to remember that usually you're not being asked to do anything new in pressurized situations. In fact, you're often doing something you've done several or even many times before, simply under pressure. Try to calm your mind as much as possible, and focus on repeating behaviours that you have done before.

Take the example of an exam. You're more likely to feel overwhelmed if you focus on how important it is, especially if you overthink all the negative ways in which failing could affect your future. Instead, focus on the fact that you're just sitting in the school hall, waiting for the chance to show what you know. Or you could treat it as a 90-minute period in which you answer questions set by a teacher, which is something you have probably been doing in class for most of your school life. Once you realize that the situation is special but not unique, you can rely on all the processes that you have practised and prepared.

It is not always straightforward to approach a pressurized situation in that way, though. Often our thoughts spiral and we freeze, or we become agitated or careless. You might start thinking about the pressure, rather than the skills you need to perform the task in hand. This is common, and something that high performers have tried to understand and overcome. The key is to understand your brain. Pressure can push your brain into a state of '**FIGHT OR FLIGHT**', which we described in the previous chapter. This describes how animal brains respond to a threat, and while it is a useful response for animals and our ancestors, it is rarely useful in the modern world. Job interviews, exams, and most challenges we face in the modern world don't give any marks for fighting or freezing.

The good thing is that the part of our brain that operates in terms of fight or flight is ancient, and through millions of years of evolution, you have developed other parts of your brain that are capable of rationalizing situations. This part of your brain separates you from animals who act on impulse. It makes you capable of creating strategies that can help you to perform. The High Performance Foundation likes to distinguish these two parts of our brain as the red and the blue brain.

The **red brain** is the part of us that responds to situations emotionally, charging us with fear or anger.

The **blue brain** is the more rational part that can get it under control.

If you can be aware of how your red brain acts under pressure, and use your blue brain to get it under control, then you have a recipe for performing at your best.

AWARENESS

If you can be aware of the times when your red brain is taking charge, you have taken the first step towards bringing your rational blue brain back into the driving seat. You have to spot when this is happening, and the easiest way is to ask yourself:

IF I WAS LOOKING AT MY SITUATION FROM THE OUTSIDE, WOULD I THINK THAT MY REACTION WAS HELPFUL?

You act, for a moment, as if you had the power to stand outside yourself and observe your thoughts, feelings, and actions. Often, this step leads to the realization that panic is not the most helpful response. Try it next time you feel you're reacting emotionally to a stressful situation. It will be the first move in allowing your blue brain to take charge again, to stop thinking like a threatened animal and start thinking like a thoughtful human. It will put you back on track and allow you to take the next step, which means using your blue brain to evaluate the challenge you have been set.

DAC – DEMANDS, ABILITY, CONSEQUENCES

You can break any challenging situation down into three parts: the demands, your ability, and the consequences. Often, when we feel overwhelmed by pressure, we allow our red brain to focus on one of these three aspects, and misrepresent it. Usually this means thinking:

THE TASK IS TOO DEMANDING.

I DON'T HAVE THE ABILITY TO COMPLETE IT.

THE CONSEQUENCES ARE SCARILY BIG.

You have to approach each aspect of your pressurized situation, in turn.

Demands	Ability	Consequences
What is actually being asked of me in the task I'm undertaking?	What skills will I need to complete it?	What are the real consequences of my failure to succeed in this endeavour? Are the consequences really as bad as I am making out?

When you apply blue-brain thinking, you usually realize that the demands are not unreasonable. An exam, for example, is a test of information that you have studied and it involves reading, writing, and timekeeping. These are all things you have done before, so you should try to remember that the demands are not new and they are not beyond you. This brings us to ability.

Your ability, if you're calmly doing your best, is enough. You are able to read, write, and manage your time, even if it is sometimes challenging. If you can do these three things, and do them with your blue brain acting rationally rather than your red brain panicking, you will do your best.

Finally, the consequences are rarely as devastating as our red brain tells us they are. This part of our mind was created to help us deal with predators, not exam papers, so it often mislabels challenges as mortal threats. The real consequences of an exam not going to plan are a retake or a change of your plans. Retakes are not comparable to sabretooth tigers – and changes of plan, as we have said, can sometimes be a new opportunity.

So it's best to get your red brain in check and reframe your situation in terms of the demands, your ability, and the consequences you might face. This allows your blue brain to take over, and you regain a sense of control. Letting your blue brain take control is the best way to stop your red brain from making you feel and behave as if you're out of control.

DEMANDS

You are also more likely to feel in control if you have visualized a stressful situation before you arrived there. All you have to do is take some time during a quiet moment to think about an event, such as an exam. You could imagine your exam room on the first day of your exams, including the chairs and tables in neat rows, the invigilator who is overseeing the exam, and the sound of footsteps crossing the sports hall floor. Then you could picture a test paper in front of you. Try to see yourself in the situation, and observe as you calmly plan out your time. Watch the best version of yourself working out a creative approach to a challenging question. See yourself *doing* your best, but calmly.

This is more than wishful thinking, or daydreaming; it is **VISUALIZING** – a practice that numerous high performers use to give themselves a head start on any challenge they may face. It allows them to approach a stressful situation and feel as though they have seen it before, as if they know what to expect. As we have said many times, the fear of the unknown is a fear that you can overcome by gaining knowledge, and because fear is an emotion that impacts performance, you can improve your outcomes by dealing with your fear.

Visualize a challenge.

Think of a challenge you will likely face in the next year.

Next, try to visualize yourself stepping into it.

Who is there? What kind of place are you in?

Finally, picture yourself doing exactly what you set out to do.

Even better, the act of visualizing can allow you to engage in deeper, clearer planning. If you were to visualize yourself and also take into account the structure of the exam paper you will take (which will be available online, or you can ask your teachers), you could work out how you were going to use your time and visualize yourself doing it. If you know the number of questions you will face, the time you have, and the marks that will be available, you will be able to break down the big challenge (the exam) into a series of smaller, time-efficient tasks. This is the act of **COMPARTMENTALIZING**.

COMPARTMENTALIZING

Compartmentalizing is a fantastic way to turn daunting challenges into a series of smaller, manageable tasks. Take this handbook. If we told you it was your job to write it, how would you feel? And, more importantly, what would you do? You might feel overwhelmed, panicked, and uncertain. You might decide that such a huge task was too much to even comprehend. Or you could have a conversation with the person who asked you to write the book. The conversation could go along these lines:

'SO THERE WOULD BE ABOUT 500 WORDS ON EACH SUBJECT. THAT'S BETTER. IS THERE INFORMATION ON THESE SUBJECTS OUT THERE?'

'YES, HIGH PERFORMANCE AND THE PSYCHOLOGY OF ELITE PERFORMERS IS VERY WELL STUDIED. THERE IS A LOT OF INFORMATION OUT THERE.'

'SO I NEED TO FIND SOME GOOD SOURCES AND WRITE NOTES ON EACH SUBJECT, ONE BY ONE. THEN I NEED TO TURN THOSE NOTES INTO 500-WORD CHUNKS, AND CONNECT THEM TOGETHER. THAT'S A MANAGEABLE TASK. I CAN DO THAT.'

See how it's possible to turn a large and potentially alarming challenge into a manageable one by breaking it down into smaller parts and accessing the relevant knowledge? This is the way people approach complex tasks in most fields. Engineers don't ask how to build a transport network. They build an engine, and connect it to the carriages and moving parts. They work out how to make these moving parts fit with tracks and lines, and then they work with those in charge of transport infrastructure to connect the tracks and power lines efficiently. The challenge of building a transport network would seem impossible if you could not break it down into its parts, or access knowledge about how the parts can fit together.

Our high performers do the same: they take their big goals and break them down into manageable steps. They learn what is required of them and realize that they are capable of doing it, because they have learned the steps that are required to complete it.

Start compartmentalizing.

Pick a task you have to complete in the coming months. Maybe it is a test, an application, or a competition.

What are the parts that make up this challenge? Break it down into as many small parts as possible.

Is any one of these parts beyond your ability?

ABILITY

So, you have learned what is being asked of you and have broken that down into manageable components, but the questions remain:

HOW DO I KNOW I'M CAPABLE OF MEETING THE REQUIREMENTS OF THESE COMPONENTS?

HOW DO I CONVINCE MYSELF WHEN DOUBT SETS IN?

This is something that British Olympic sprinter Dina Asher-Smith struggled with early in her career. She is one of the country's greatest-ever sprinters, but before she became a champion she was a young person who was undermined by her fear of failure. Dina knew clearly what was expected of her, but she doubted her ability. In the World Athletics Championships semi-final in 2019, she had a poor start but still managed to qualify for the final. Dina knew that if she had such a poor start in the final, she would fail to achieve her goal. Panic and doubt set in, and her red brain was activated.

The problem was that Dina's panic was a near-certain route to failure. In a race of seconds and small margins, worrying about a bad start is a **SELF-FULFILLING PROPHECY** – the most likely way to make one happen. You can become too adrenalized, then react too fast, and move before the gun fires. This is a false start, and false starts mean disqualification. Or, instead of a false start, your worry makes you start slowly. Dina's mind would focus on the possibility of her failure rather than the very real challenge of getting out of the blocks faster than her opponents. The milliseconds that she spent in anxious thought would be the difference between a good start and a slow start. She would start poorly *because* she feared starting poorly.

Dina decided to speak to her coach. She suggested to him that they spend the days before the final practising starts, over and over again. She would have to learn to start all over again, just two days before the race of her life. Her coach disagreed. He thought that this was a poor use of time considering that he had seen her start quickly hundreds of times. She hadn't forgotten how to start well; she had forgotten *that she already knew* how to start well. The slow start was the exception, not the rule. 'You're going to go out there and just do your normal start,' he told her. 'That is all you're going to do... the normal start you have done thousands of times before.'

He knew that, within Dina, she already had what she needed to win. She simply had to see it, and seeing it meant letting her blue brain take control of the red. So she did, and with her blue brain in charge and her coach's words still ringing in her ears, she started well, as she had done so many times before. She won the gold medal.

You must always try to **focus** on the **reality of your challenge**, not the catastrophe you imagine.

The energy you spend thinking about an imaginary problem often *is* the problem. If it is an exam, you should remind yourself how many tests you have done already, how many questions you have answered, and words you have written. If it is a big interview, you should think about how many conversations you have had in your life. A conversation is something that you know how to do, and it only seems unmanageable if you convince yourself that *this conversation* is somehow different to all the others that you've ever had, and that you therefore lack the ability to take it on.

You have the ability to meet your challenges, but you must keep your challenges in perspective and your sense of your own ability close at hand.

Create a confidence bank account.

Take a moment to catalogue your skills. Think about them just like a **confidence bank account** that you can top up whenever you want – for free. This account will be a great resource for when your red brain tries to take over.

Professional golfer Matt Fitzpatrick told us that he records every shot he plays and then returns to watch the best ones when he needs a confidence boost. Your list, like his videos, offers something to look back on when you need reminding that you are more capable than your stressed mind is letting you believe. Ask yourself these questions:

WHAT AM I GREAT AT?

WHAT SKILLS DO I HAVE?

MOST IMPORTANTLY, WHAT IS IT THAT I SIMPLY KNOW I CAN DO?

These might seem like small things, such as greeting people and holding a conversation, but it is worth remembering that these are still skills, and you have them.

This is a good way to build up a secure base of **SELF-BELIEF**, but you will grow even more confident if you also take time to consider the skills you have showcased through your achievements. Every time you have achieved something, you have relied on a diverse set of skills, including hard work, determination, resilience, focus, and teamwork, and you should never take these skills for granted.

Next time you achieve something, try to recall in detail how you achieved it. Consider how you were feeling while you pursued the challenge, what you were thinking, and how you behaved. Remember the moments when you felt doubt or fear in the run-up to a task, but overcame them and completed it. Think back to them when you face your next challenge. Maybe you successfully navigated your first day at sixth form. How did you feel the night before? What did you do on the day? And how do you feel it went? You made it through that day, and you should think about how.

Here's another example: maybe you cooked a meal for your family or friends. What were the steps?

These achievements will follow the same structure as every challenge you face for the rest of your life, so it is worth taking them into account.

There was a **demand.**

You used your **ability.**

And there was a **consequence.**

You had something you needed or wanted to do, you committed to doing it, and then you did it. Even the smallest tasks will follow that structure, and being aware of the way in which you navigated them will give you greater self-belief when you face bigger ones.

CONSEQUENCES

The final component of a good strategy in the face of pressure involves the ability to understand consequences. While an appreciation of consequences is necessary for future planning, a focus on imagined ones is a sure-fire way to undermine our chances of success.

The tendency to focus on imaginary consequences is known as **CATASTROPHIZING**. It impacts your ability to meet challenges because it takes a small challenge that you can manage and makes it seem like a big one that you cannot overcome. We can all do an exam, but no one can control an imagined situation where everything in our lives falls apart because we have failed. The problem is that our catastrophes are, by definition, greater than our ability to devise solutions. They are imaginary and, because of that, they have no limits.

You have to retain your focus on what a task really is and what the *actual* consequences are. As we've mentioned, a failed exam may mean a retake, or it may mean a change in plans or career path, but it might prove to be an opportunity. It is not a catastrophe, and it is not going to mean your whole life will fall apart. You have to take charge of any catastrophic thoughts, both for your happiness and your effectiveness.

Energy spent on a hypothetical **worst-case outcome** could just as easily be spent thinking about a hypothetical **best-case scenario.**

Perhaps a failed exam could lead you to join a local television station instead of going to university. Maybe that could lead to a career as a respected, national broadcaster. It is possible that you could end up creating an interview format with high performers. This is exactly what happened to Jake Humphrey. His catastrophe turned out to be an opportunity, so it would be just as sensible to spend our precious mental energy thinking about all of the ways in which a failed exam could be great, as it is to think about the ways in which it could be terrible.

The best approach, of course, is to do neither, and try to be realistic about consequences. You're unlikely to experience a chain of entirely negative impacts from a disappointment, and equally unlikely to experience only positives. You're likely to experience reality, which is a mixture of good and bad, and not always in your control. So you should think about what reality might look like and what you might be able to do if your original plan fails. Most likely, you will discover this:

Even the worst-case scenario is **well within your abilities** to overcome.

As Laila Ali put it: 'You're never going to be faced with something harder than you can actually overcome.'

The greatest English rugby player of his generation learned about overcoming disappointments the hard way. Jonny Wilkinson scored the winning points in England's only ever World Cup win, and yet he spent most of his career focusing on his disappointments, and the catastrophes that might be waiting for him in the next game. For many years, Jonny never experienced the joy of playing and succeeding at the highest level because his mind was consumed with imagined future mistakes. He was overcome by a fear of the shame and ridicule that he might experience.

So he decided that he needed to change his perspective by separating his identity from his achievements. Jonny made a conscious decision to develop a core positive view of himself that didn't change whether he played well or badly. He would no longer get too high when things went well or too low when they didn't because he remained the same. The benefit of this approach is as follows:

You can **treat** your **disappointments** as **events**, not evidence of flaws.

You free yourself from concerns about what people will think of you when you fail and gain perspective of the consequences. You learn that even the most consequential event can't change how you view yourself.

This is called an **INTERNAL LOCUS OF EVALUATION**. 'Locus' means a place or centre, so this just means that this sense of evaluation is within *you*. It means deciding on your own standards and your own way of evaluating your performance. It is not tied to the opinions of others or the results you achieve but your own effort. If you can genuinely say you have done your best, you can be confident that you will be satisfied. Even a disappointment is a victory if you have met your own standards of effort and application. This allows you to learn how you can do better when you fail to meet your own standards – and, unlike living by external standards, it is entirely within your control.

Bad luck or harsh judges cannot change how you feel. Consequences become predictable and manageable because you are your best and only judge. You either win and feel pride, or lose and learn.

Usain Bolt received this advice from his coach Glen Mills: 'You have to learn how to lose before you can learn how to win.' He admits that it took him two years to figure out what that meant, but he eventually understood that if you can be truthful to yourself when you lose and ask, 'What did I do wrong? What do I need to improve?' then you can learn from your failures.

You will be glad to know that an internal locus of evaluation is both a result and a driver of blue-brain thinking. You can perform better and feel less pressure when you're the judge of your own performance. You can always rest assured that you know what it takes to meet your own standards, and that will result in a more consistent and less stressful life.

Think of a time when you tried to achieve something and didn't succeed.

Picture how you would react to that situation with two different mindsets.

One is an external focus, where most of your thoughts are about how other people perceive you, and the other is with your own internal locus of evaluation, where you are mostly judging your own effort.

What did you find out when you judged your own effort? Did you think you could have done more – and could therefore learn something from it? Or did you think that you did your best and couldn't control the outcome? Both these observations are better than thinking about external judgement.

STRESS

Stress is the product of letting your red brain take over your blue brain for long periods of time. The mental health charity Mind defines it, on their website, as this:

> **Stress** is how we react when we feel under pressure or threatened. It usually happens when we are in a situation that we don't feel we can manage or control.

Here we see our old friends pressure and control returning again. The greatest response to pressure is a sense of control, and a sense of control is exactly what separates a stressful situation from a satisfying challenge. This is why you must think again about how you maintain a sense of control in response to short- or long-term pressure, as that is the best way to keep the feeling of stress at bay. Fortunately, the short-term strategies we have discussed for approaching pressurized situations can be applied in the longer term to manage stress.

For example, we use awareness of our thoughts and feelings to understand whether our red brain is dominant in pressurized situations, but you can also use this awareness to understand your thoughts and feelings in the long term. During a stressful period, it is helpful to check in with yourself and develop an awareness of how you're feeling day to day. There are benefits to keeping a daily journal:

- You can monitor your stress levels and the broader state of your emotions.
- You can learn to understand the events that make you feel more or less stressed on any given day.
- Recording the events, and your thoughts and feelings for the day can be a relaxing process in itself.

The self-awareness that you build allows you to focus on trademark behaviours that reduce stress and to consider removing habits that increase stress. In addition, this awareness increases your sense of control, which is the overall aim of any stress management approach.

For Tom Grennan, writing down his thoughts helped him to communicate his feelings after he was randomly attacked in the street at the age of 18, which resulted in him needing surgery. A few years later, Tom returned to his notebooks, and his words became the basis of the first songs that he wrote.

A journal can be as simple or as detailed as you like, but many people choose to complete them either at night before bed or in the morning when they wake up. It should include some details of the things you did that day or the day before, the feelings you experienced, and some deliberately positive thoughts, such as **AFFIRMATIONS** or **GRATITUDE LISTS**. Laila Ali acknowledges that you might not feel like you have anything positive to say, but 'put in the work so you can feel good about yourself'.

Affirmations are a form of **SELF-TALK**. They allow us to approach ourselves more like a kind, supportive friend rather than a teasing, taunting enemy that an anxious mind can feel like. A stressed and anxious mind may seem to be constantly tugging at your sleeve, telling you that you are not good enough, but an affirmative mind will remark on how well you did, the efforts you made, and the positivity you spread in the world.

We use affirmations to *train* our minds to be kind to ourselves. Former lawyer and author Mel Robbins told us about how she developed a practice of high-fiving herself in the mirror each morning as a way to help her self-awareness and appreciation. Thoughts are flexible, and if you actively choose to engage in positive self-talk, you will generally be kinder to yourself. This, in itself, is a reminder of the control that you have, and therefore a healthy response to stress.

A gratitude list is less about how you think about yourself and more about how you think about the world. Consider these two key components of how you feel about your life:

AM I KIND TO MYSELF?

DO I FEEL THAT THE WORLD IS A GOOD PLACE?

Again, you can assert control and make yourself feel more positively about the world through the practice of writing a gratitude list. At the end of your journal entry, you have to actively think of three things you are grateful for that day. These may be things like a warm bed to sleep in, the people that love you, or an unexpected smile from someone you met. Anything that you can feel grateful for is worthy of your gratitude list, and taking time to note such a thing has a profound psychological impact.

One of the most powerful aspects of practising gratitude is that it not only allows us to appreciate the good things in our everyday lives, but trains us to find light even in our darkest moments. Fundraising campaigner Lindsey Burrow told us about how she continued to practise gratitude after her husband, Rob, passed away. The rugby league legend died of the degenerative condition motor neurone disease. She had learned to be grateful, and it allowed her to experience positivity and joy even in the most difficult circumstances. It cannot be overstated how incredible this response is, and how valuable this can be for all of us, given that we will all experience loss, grief, and adversity in our lives. Gratitude is a superpower that we can all develop.

The more grateful you feel for the situation you're in, the more you will be able to enjoy your life and the small, good things that come your way every day. So, together with your words of affirmation, you can develop a mindset that is kind to yourself and grateful for your life. This combination of kindness and gratitude is a great way to develop a positive, stress-free, and high-performing mind. Best of all, as you enjoy the benefits of these practices, you will increase your sense of control over your mind and your reactions to the world around you.

Words of affirmation.

Write an affirmation. Something kind and supportive about yourself, such as 'I make an effort for my friends.'

Write a list of three things you are grateful for today.

These forms of awareness tie in with our DAC (demand, ability, and consequences) model, which is just as useful for managing stress as it is for pressure. Kind self-talk is key to developing a sense of your abilities, and stopping you from engaging in red-brained criticisms of your own capability.

Gratitude helps us develop a realistic sense of the world, and its demands and consequences. If you have gratitude, you gain balance, and see that the world is both demanding and rewarding. This allows you to take control of your red brain when it starts telling you the world is full of unreasonable demands, or spiralling, catastrophic consequences.

BE YOUR OWN JUDGE

You should gain security from the idea that applying the DAC model allows you to manage long-term stress as well as short-term pressure. When you're feeling stressed over a period of time, it is helpful to ask yourself what is being demanded of you. Often our stress is based on imagined, inflated demands that we create for ourselves. Ideas such as 'I have to be perfect' make us feel a great deal of stress in everything we do, as each moment is an opportunity for us to fail to meet our demands. By considering the broader demands we set for ourselves, we can often redirect them into goals or behaviours, and take back control.

The unrealistic demands we create may also be tied to stressful and painful imaginary consequences. The demand 'I have to be perfect' only has power if you tie it to the consequence of being 'worthwhile', or 'worthy of love'. Many of us assume that our value is tied to our ability or achievements, and that attaches each of these things to consequences that can feel terrifying. We will all fail sometimes, and you will be no less worthy of love if you do, so you have to develop a strong sense of the consequences of your actions in the long term.

It is only then – through an understanding of the demands you impose on yourself and the consequences that you attach to them – that you can arrive at a healthy sense of your abilities. Stress and a lack of control are feelings you experience when you're stretched between what is demanded of you and the catastrophic consequences of failing to meet those demands.

If you believe that you must be perfect, and that you will be unworthy of love if you're not, then you will often doubt your ability to meet the demands and fear the consequences. So, you should explore why you believe you should be perfect, and remind yourself that you're worthwhile even when you fail to achieve perfection.

You are your only judge and **you know better** than anyone else whether you have performed at the level you expect of yourself.

This type of self-evaluation will also help you to lead a less stressful life. If you can evaluate your own performance by your own standards, there is less room to be caught up in the need for things like perfection or validation from others, and less reason to doubt your ability to meet those standards. If you are your own best judge, you are in control of your standards and your performance, and you won't need to doubt your ability. Most importantly, if you have worked on a practice of self-compassion by writing your journal, then you can be a strong but fair judge.

Finally, many high performers come to the realization that stress is both a mental and physical phenomenon. Stress triggers changes in our bodies, but a healthy body can also change our relationship with stress. So gain control over your stress level by treating physical health, nutrition, and exercise as levers you can pull to manage your stress.

In the previous chapter, we discussed how exercise helps us to deal with anxiety, but we should also consider how the food we eat affects our mental health. Dr Chris van Tulleken spoke to us about how eating ultra-processed foods can have a negative impact on our mental health, and in turn, how adopting a diet full of natural fruits, vegetables, and grains can have a positive effect on our minds. Sometimes, we don't have many options at home or with school lunches, and it's important that we still eat something to nourish our bodies. However, having this understanding helps a lot of people to make better food choices, as the difference between choosing a pack of sweets and a banana can be made clearer when we realize that we are eating for both our mental and physical health. High performers achieve high-quality outputs, and it is crucial to understand that this is driven by high-quality inputs, such as natural, nutrient-rich foods.

SLEEP

Consistent sleep is key to managing your mental wellbeing. If we were to recommend a single physical and mental health intervention to get you on a high-performance track, it would be the development of a healthy sleep schedule. Go to bed at the same time each night and wake up at the same time every morning. This not only gives you a sense of control, but it affects so many of your health-promoting behaviours. Research has shown that people make better nutrition choices after a good sleep. You can work more effectively after rest, and you can think more clearly.

Creating a sleep routine is something you have a lot of control over, and it also makes you more capable of feeling in control in every moment that you're awake.

Set yourself a bedtime ritual and stick to it.

Set your wake-up time in advance and keep it consistent.

Wind down before you go to bed, ideally for the last couple of hours.

Make sure that the lights around you are reduced or dimmer, if possible.

Avoid the sort of activities that make your brain feel busy or active. This means anything with screens, and particularly things like games that are designed to activate your dopamine reward system.

Although the dopamine system sounds like a complex idea, it's actually really straightforward. Your dopamine system is the reward system in your brain. It developed as a way for our brain to tell us that we had found something good, like a high-energy food source, or that we had achieved something difficult, such as running for a long time. The challenge is that in the modern world, many things that trigger our dopamine system are now available round the clock. Scrolling social media, eating sugary foods, and online shopping all activate it. These things give us a sense of reward, but because they are not tied to genuine effort, they are not truly rewarding. You have to be very conscious of activating your dopamine system, because the more you use it for these easy things, the less you will be able to turn to it for motivation for more difficult things. Activating it too much will also affect your ability to concentrate and to sleep. So try not to engage in dopamine-spiking behaviours, such as social media or video games, in the hours before bed or before a time when you have to focus. It will only set your brain up to whizz and whir and look for distractions that offer dopamine.

It's necessary to train your mind to attach dopamine rewards to hard things. If you can do difficult, challenging things and feel rewarded by them, you can increase your motivation and develop a more balanced dopamine system. This means that you're less likely to go searching for it, and less likely to get caught up in addictive habits. Exercise – in particular cardio exercise – is a great way to balance your dopamine system. Cardio exercise, such as running or cycling, raises your heart rate and gives you a dopamine release (reward) that lasts throughout the day. This means you're not as likely to go searching for activities that give you short, sharp spikes of dopamine, which leave you feeling unfulfilled. You will be more capable of enjoying the small, simple things in everyday life instead of looking for a dopamine hit from one of the many addictive sources that are available to us in the modern world. Boxer Tyson Fury told us that he broke through a cycle of addiction by exercising and focusing on enjoying the small pleasures in his day – everything including a trip to the rubbish dump was something to be enjoyed!

BUILD YOUR STRESS-RELEASE TOOLKIT

Make sure you add exercise to your toolbox for dealing with stress, alongside good sleep, and mindfulness practices such as gratitude and journalling. The result is that you will have a set of lifestyle choices that can help to manage stress and make you feel in control of your situation in the long term. Your toolkit also includes short-term approaches that help you when you're feeling under pressure.

Stress is something that you want to minimize every day, so developing a healthy lifestyle is vital, but pressure is something that you cannot control in quite the same way. When it comes to pressure, it is your response to it that you must manage and, although the general approaches for dealing with stress are relevant, it is important to keep in mind the specific techniques you can use when facing pressure. So let's recap.

You experience pressure when you take on worthwhile challenges and seek opportunities, so it is better to deal with it and maintain your performance even when the pressure is on. You must also learn to manage your emotions, and looking at yourself from the outside is a great way to tell whether you're letting your emotional red brain take over from the rational blue one. Remember, your first response to a pressurized situation should be to:

- Evaluate the demands: what is being asked of you?
- Consider your abilities: remembering all that you're capable of.
- List the realistic consequences: they will rarely be as scary as they seemed at first glance.
- Focus on the fact that you're the only judge that matters.

If you have worked hard and continue doing your best with your blue brain in charge, you have nothing to worry about. The only outcomes are success, or an opportunity to learn and do better next time.

So try to appreciate pressure – see it as the necessary price you pay for achievements, and remember that a life without it would not be one that you would want. Seek opportunities and the pressure that comes with them, confident in the knowledge that you have the resources to remain in control and respond at your best.

Learning to control the controllables and to be your own judge are important steps in your journey towards high performance.

KEY TAKEAWAYS

1. A life without pressure is like a footballer without a cup final or a performer without an audience. It's a privilege.
2. Use adrenaline to power you, but do not let it take over. You are in control.
3. Be conscious of your red brain and your blue brain. Your red brain feels, while your blue brain thinks.
4. Look at yourself and ask yourself: Is my reaction to pressure helping me? How can I get my blue brain in charge?
5. In moments of stress or pressure, understand the demands, your ability, and the consequences.
6. Focus on how the demands are achievable, your ability is enough, and the consequences manageable.
7. Break down your task into manageable components.
8. Develop a sense of yourself as your own judge.
9. Keep a journal, write gratitude lists, sleep and eat well, and exercise. These will all help you to manage stress, face pressure, and feel healthier while you do.

5

CLEARING HURDLES

WE ALL FACE setbacks, and we all have hurdles we must clear on the path to our goals. These hurdles can be large or small, and they can come from outside or from within your own mind, but only you have the power to overcome them. Only you have the power to control how you react, and only you have the power to develop a resilient and optimistic mind for yourself.

One day you're going to experience disappointment, and you're going to fail. Everyone we have spoken to on our podcast – no matter how many gold medals or World Cups they have won – has lost at some point in their life. However, they have never been beaten.

> To lose is **human,**
> but it's also an **event.**

To feel like you've been beaten is to accept defeat and give up on the possibility of a future victory – and that feeling is a choice.

To develop the mindset of a winner and a learner (for a high performer, these are the only two options – no losses, only lessons), you have to make a few distinctions. You have to distinguish between small and large setbacks; you have to determine what is in your control and what isn't; and you have to know the difference between positive and negative ways of thinking. If you can learn to do these three things, then you will remain in control as you try to achieve your goals.

So, how do you deal with small setbacks? These are frustrations, annoyances, or difficulties that are more like distractions than serious challenges, but that doesn't mean they should be ignored. If you let small setbacks get the better of you, they will become bigger problems further down the line.

This is something that Dutch football star Robin van Persie struggled with early in his career. He discussed with us his journey from upcoming talent to high performer, and much like fellow footballer Rio Ferdinand, he had to overcome distractions to achieve his potential. Unlike Rio, Robin's distractions were on the pitch, rather than off it. During games, he regularly found himself feeling frustrated about things he couldn't control, such as unfair refereeing decisions, annoying opponents, or aggressive opposition fans. Any of these external factors were enough to make Robin lose his focus and drop his performance level.

The problem was that all his energy was going into things he couldn't do anything about rather than using his ability to succeed in everything he could control. It created a **CYCLE OF PESSIMISM** in which the way he approached each new game was affected by the pessimism he felt in response to the last one.

A cycle of pessimism turns one problem into a journey of disappointment.

For Robin, everything changed when he realized that high performance is as much about what you don't focus on as what you do. It is about controlling the controllables and placing a full stop after your frustrations.

How do I make sure I feel *in control*? Well, the short answer is that you have to keep reminding yourself that you *are in control*. The easiest way to do this is to avoid patterns of thinking that encourage the opposite, and in particular negative thoughts that see problems as **PERVASIVE**, **PERMANENT**, or **PERSONAL**.

PERVASIVE THINKING

This is when you take a single problem and take it to mean that everything has gone or will go wrong. Say you woke up late, missed your bus to the library, and now you have to start revising an hour later than planned. A person who falls into a pattern of pervasive thoughts might say, 'Everything is going wrong.' This use of the word 'everything' turns a small setback into a large one and impacts how you think about *everything*. This type of thinking also makes people feel out of control. If everything is going wrong, then there is *nothing* you can do about it. In contrast, the situation you actually face after missing the bus only involves one problem, which is that you will arrive at the library later than planned. When you use the word 'everything', though, you trick yourself into believing that your problems extend beyond the single, manageable problem, which you could solve by revising at home first. You turn a single problem into a belief about your whole situation and lose control.

So next time you find yourself using a pervasive phrase to describe your problem, such as 'totally', 'everybody', 'no one', or 'completely', see if you can respond by asking yourself whether this is really true.

ARE MY PLANS 'TOTALLY RUINED' OR IS THERE A WORKAROUND?

DOES EVERYBODY HATE ME? OR DID ONE PERSON SAY SOMETHING UNKIND?

DOES NO ONE BELIEVE IN ME? OR DID SOMEONE DOUBT ME?

In all these instances, you can choose to think about a single problem, rather than create a belief about the whole world. A single problem is something you can control, whereas a whole world of them is beyond even the most capable high performer.

PERMANENCE

Another problem we create for ourselves is treating a problem as one that will exist forever or always. When we do this, we make the mistake of applying an idea of **PERMANENCE**. This means using phrases like 'always' or 'never' and turning something that is difficult in the moment into a belief about how things will always be.

In this list of phrases, the left-hand side shows examples of permanence thinking, and they are dangerous because they make people feel trapped and unable to control or change their situation. So, when facing a problem, switch the permanence phrases to the ones on the right and see how the difference makes you feel.

I NEVER GET THINGS RIGHT. VS I SOMETIMES GET THINGS WRONG.

THIS ALWAYS HAPPENS TO ME. VS THIS RECENTLY HAPPENED TO ME.

I CONSTANTLY HAVE NO ENERGY. VS I'VE HAD NO ENERGY LATELY.

The phrase 'I always fail science tests' is very different from 'I have failed some science tests recently'. The first phrase suggests that you will always fail them in the future, and that is far more likely if you keep telling yourself it is true. It is also simply not true. There will have been science tests you have not failed, and only by getting to the root of why you failed in the ones you did will you be able to act differently and change the outcome. Maybe the subject has grown more challenging and you need support to understand the concepts. This is fine, and there are plenty of things you can do to fix it. Maybe you have been focusing more on other subjects and you need to spend more time on science. But this is OK – it's a time-management issue, and it is within your control.

Nothing is *always* the case except for a few laws of physics, so it really doesn't help to treat our problems as particularly permanent. The final P that magnifies our problems is taking them...

PERSONALLY

When you face a setback and assume it is the result of a fundamental issue with yourself as an individual, you are taking it personally. If you ever catch yourself making a mistake and saying 'I'm stupid', then you have room to grow in this area because when you heap blame on yourself, you multiply the pain. There is the issue of the problem itself, and then all the negative emotions that you layer onto yourself as well. Yes, you should take responsibility for your mistakes, but if you waste energy beating yourself up over them, you won't have many internal resources left to fix them.

Reserve your energy for solutions and progress, not harsh self-talk.

This is **NEGATIVE LABELLING** and it won't help.

High performance is about taking responsibility for the things you do, and in a way taking things personally is the opposite of that. It assumes you're powerless to change events and leaves no option to change yourself or the outcome of a future situation. You will see as we go forward that high performers face many difficult situations and make many mistakes, but they focus on learning from them, taking responsibility, and dealing with their outcomes.

OWN YOUR MISTAKES

We all make mistakes. Every high performer we have interviewed has, and you will too, but the way in which we make mistakes and the ways we respond to them drive many aspects of high performance. There are two crucial components to committing an error *effectively*, and these are:

- Being able to **acknowledge it**.

- Being able to **learn from it**.

The first aspect is not as simple as it seems. Many people prefer to deflect their mistakes, blame other people, or find excuses. This happens because people lack the psychological security to admit when they have gone wrong. Psychological security is the product of an environment where we feel comfortable taking risks by trying and failing and making mistakes, as well as a mindset that appreciates their value. Studies have consistently shown that businesses and teams with a high degree of psychological safety outperform those with less, and in large part this is because people are free to try new and challenging approaches, and to admit when things have gone wrong.

This is powerful because admitting you have gone wrong is the first step in learning *why* this happened and ensuring that you perform better the next time. We learn as much from what doesn't work as what does, if we have developed the right mindset of psychological security. So, own your mistakes and understand that they are as key to your long-term success as your individual victories.

FACING SETBACKS BEYOND YOUR CONTROL

We learn from our mistakes by taking responsibility, but often the setbacks we experience are beyond our control. Maybe you get injured the week before a cup final, or you get sick during the week of exams. You've done nothing wrong, yet you have suffered, so what do you do? Do you focus on how unfair it is that you were injured when other players who don't train as hard get to play in the final? Do you focus on how it is *just your luck* to get sick? Or do you accept that the situation is beyond your control and then think about the things that are within your control?

High performers understand that setbacks are part of everyone's experience, but it is their response that will make the difference. You can think of this in terms of an equation.

Life + Response = Outcome

You cannot always control the events that make up your life. People get sick, cars break down, and sometimes all the bad things seem to happen at the worst time, but you can control how you respond – and the outcome will rest entirely on that.

No matter how terrible life events are, positive outcomes can be found if you come up with the right response. This was never more clear than in our conversation with racing driver Billy Monger. In 2017 he was competing in a British Formula 4 race at Donnington Park. He was 17 and had a bright future ahead of him in motorsport. Without his knowledge, a car up ahead had slowed down, and his view of it was obscured by his fellow racers that he was overtaking. By the time he had a chance to brake, it was too late, and he crashed into the back of a car, spinning off the track. Billy was rushed to hospital and placed in an induced coma for five weeks. When he woke, he discovered that both his legs had been amputated at the knee. This is a moment when an event has the potential to overwhelm our response to it. For Billy, though, it was not.

'I knew it was not my fault, but how I reacted was my responsibility,' he told us. Those words carry some very important ideas. You can always distinguish between a mistake and a misfortune. By saying that it was not his fault, Billy accepted that what had happened was unfortunate, but that it was not something that he felt responsible for. In a tragic situation like this, there is no room for self-blame or learning – only acceptance. What happened was a reality beyond his control, and because he accepted it, he was free to think about how he would respond to it. He chose to focus on his physiotherapy and to find an adapted car, and within 11 weeks he was back behind the wheel racing again.

We see in Billy's example that taking responsibility for his response to misfortune was not some sort of moral idea of what is right or wrong. It was not philosophical; it was practical. It was the best thing for him. He could have spent 11 weeks dwelling on every moment that had led to the accident, or wondering what his life would be like if it had not occurred, but instead he focused on what he could do and discovered that there were outcomes in which he could still do the things he loved. As it turned out, the greatest tragedy would not have been his accident, but it would have been what happened if he had allowed it to turn his life into a tragedy.

Making choices like this shows us how important our response to setbacks can be, but they also put our own setbacks in perspective. We are reminded that our problems are not the greatest that anyone has ever suffered, and just as we can ask 'Why me?' in response to hardship, we could also ask 'Why not me?' when it comes to all the difficult things people across the world are experiencing. This awareness of other people's difficulties can free us from the personal and pervasive lines of thinking that we described earlier. If Billy could regain control and perspective, so can you.

SETBACKS CAN BE NEW BEGINNINGS

Celebrated percussionist Evelyn Glennie told us the story of how she lost her hearing and became a musician.

Evelyn has been deaf since the age of 12. In a music lesson soon after she lost her hearing, her teacher played an instrument and asked her if she could *feel* the sound. She paused, let her mind's ear travel inside, and decided that yes, she could. Evelyn decided not to focus on her deafness, which is an aspect of her life beyond her control, but on how she could achieve the outcome of being a musician without hearing, and that set her up to discover approaches and responses that allowed her to play music. In her words, 'This is the scenario – that's what needs to happen, and it makes absolutely no difference to the quality of the end product.' She decided to tweak her behaviour in response by doing things like facing fellow musicians at 90-degree angles to feel the music better; she chose to develop her awareness of sound. Evelyn realized that she needed to approach music differently from people who were not deaf, but that she did not need to give up on it.

This demonstrates an important way in which high performers tackle setbacks – they look at their situation and they decide on ways to do things differently. In many cases, it is precisely doing things differently that allows them to be innovative. Sometimes we are pushed to work in new ways, and often new ways of working are better than the old assumptions.

Setbacks can push you towards new and better ways of thinking and working, but they can also teach you resilience. It is recognized that hardships build strength, just as heavy weights build muscle, and someone who knows a lot about both those things is rugby player Siya Kolisi.

The two-times Rugby World Cup-winning captain is a champion, and in our conversations he argued that his hardships and those of his teammates were pivotal to their success. Many international rugby teams draw their players from middle-class communities. Unlike boxing or football, it is not generally a sport that is played by working-class people, with some exceptions. However, the South African rugby team captained by Siya was different. Unlike the Springboks of the past, his team was drawn from across South African society, with many individuals who had grown up in some of the country's poorest communities. For Siya, the presence of players who had known the true hardship of poverty gave his team a strength and perspective that put them at an advantage. His teammates knew what it was like to walk for miles to access water, or to struggle to get enough food each day. These experiences had taught them what true pressure really was, and not even a Rugby World Cup final could match it. To them, the great challenge and opportunity of a final in front of 80,000 people was something they were prepared for, and they had been prepared for it by the experience of what they had gone through already in life.

Like Billy and Evelyn, Siya had seen that hardship was beyond his control, but that through a thoughtful response there were ways to turn it into strength. These three high performers prove that resilience is powerful but accessible to us all. It is the ability to accept that disappointing and sometimes terrible things are a part of life.

> You can't change what has already happened, but you **can** think about what you can change **going forward.**

Whether that means learning from your hardship, doing the same thing *better*, or pivoting towards a new challenge, you'll be safe in the knowledge that you have the strength to respond, recover, and grow from setbacks.

HOW YOU PIVOT

Evelyn Glennie successfully pivoted from one approach to another when she lost her hearing. She learned to listen in a new way. Billy Monger did the same, finding a different approach to racing at a high level as an amputee. Although we might have made pivoting sound straightforward, it definitely wasn't. Evelyn and Billy had to start somewhere, though, and then move forward – and the first step they took was *believing* that their problems could be overcome.

SELF-BELIEF is the first step to problem-solving. If you do not think you have what it takes to clear a hurdle, then you will not be able to take the steps to do it. You have to believe that you can learn and grow in order to overcome your problems. Self-belief is believing that you can grow and that you can learn enough to achieve things that you can't currently.

This is the idea of a **GROWTH MINDSET**.

Put simply, a growth mindset is the belief that you are the sort of person who can overcome challenges. Self-belief, though, is the opposite of thinking that you're good at something. Take the example of a maths test and a student who is 'good at maths' but who lacks a growth mindset. They may complete the questions that are within their ability range, but when they get to questions that stretch them or require them to improve their skills, they might become frustrated and give up. In contrast, a person who has a growth mindset but lacks the traditional aptitude for maths may be challenged by each question, but they will see themselves as someone who is 'good at overcoming challenges'. For them, each question is an opportunity to learn and to grow, and, as a result, no question is too hard or too frustrating – it's just another opportunity. While the person who is 'good at maths' finds that their identity is challenged when presented with a difficult maths question, the self-believer actually has their identity re-enforced. A fixed mindset is fragile, whereas a growth mindset makes anything possible.

Psychologist Carol Dweck first came up with the idea of a growth mindset while working in schools, and she found that those pupils who had developed it were able to learn and progress faster than their peers, even when their natural academic abilities seemed to be lower. Unlike innate abilities that we are born with, a growth mindset can be learned, and for something so powerful it is surprisingly simple to do. It is so simple, you may not believe it, *yet*.

There it is.

Did you see it?

No?

Well, the trick is to add three little letters to the end of any sentence that describes our challenges: 'Y', 'E', and 'T'. When you find yourself thinking something is impossible, the addition of the word 'yet' can transform your doubts.

'I can't do algebra... yet.'

'I can't get a nine in history... yet.'

This one word can change your mindset subtly, and that small change is transformative. It gives you greater confidence and a sense that the future could be positive if you apply yourself. It creates a bridge over your dead ends and tunnels beneath those walls that seem to block your path; it is as close to magic as a single word can be.

And yet...

It's not magic – it's logical. A growth mindset plays into an idea that we have described in different ways at many points in this book, and that is **SELF-EFFICACY**. This is the idea that you are in control of your future, and you can make changes. When we spoke about Life + Response, we were talking about building self-efficacy. When we discussed the challenge of pervasive thinking (that *everything* is going wrong), we were looking at a pattern of thought that removes our sense of self-efficacy. When we spoke about making choices about the sort of person we want to be, you guessed it, that was about self-efficacy.

The sense that you are in control of your responses and your future is at the heart of high performance in so many ways, and it is no wonder that research has shown it to significantly increase our chances in life. Having a strong sense of control over our lives has 'been linked with academic success, higher self-motivation and social maturity, lower incidences of stress and depression, and a longer life span', according to journalist and author Charles Duhigg in *Smarter Faster Better: The Secrets of Being Productive*. In short, you're likely to be happier, more successful, and live longer if you decide that you're in control. It doesn't seem like a bad idea.

Think of something that you'd like to achieve, but can't do. Now add the word 'yet'. How are your feelings about that thing different now that you have applied the magic of a growth mindset?

SETBACKS AS OPPORTUNITIES

A sense of self-efficacy and a growth mindset can open us up to new opportunities in the wake of setbacks. This positive form of thinking is so powerful it can turn bad things into good ones, and again, we have to stress, it's not actually magic.

Ballet dancer Marcelino Sambé told us that one of the most important moments on his path to success was... getting injured. This was certainly a surprise. When we are asked to create a roadmap to success, we tend to only think of the good things, our talents and opportunities, the training and the progress, but here we were being told that an injury taught him how to dance. After Evelyn explained how losing her hearing taught her to listen, maybe we shouldn't have been surprised.

Marcelino explained how this injury early in his career stopped him from being able to dance or do the sort of physical training that would allow him to improve as a ballet dancer. So far, not so good for his ballet career. And yet... it seemed to benefit him in many ways. He spent nine months recovering and in those months, he decided to focus on learning about everything *around* ballet. He looked at modern art and drag performance; he thought about beauty itself and how to create a scene. Not dancing gave him a chance to become the dancer that he would otherwise never have been. He had to experience a world outside ballet to learn new perspectives that could elevate his performance. He stepped outside it, and when he returned he brought back something new.

Learning from your setbacks.

Think about a setback in your own life.

What did you learn from it?

If nothing comes to mind immediately, try to think back to the last time you wanted something but didn't get it, or had something happen that you wish had gone differently. At the very least you learned that you can experience setbacks and continue. Maybe you learned that you are resilient, and that particular setback could not break you. Maybe you learned how to avoid that problem in the future. Any negative experience can teach us powerful lessons that generate positive outcomes. You just have to take a moment to think differently about what they might be.

THINKING FLEXIBLY

The challenge is that we are often trained to think about setbacks only as events that *set us back* – whereas it only takes a small mental shift to open up to setbacks as opportunities, to treat injuries as a chance for growth, and endings as beginnings. The structure of the word 'setback' may encourage us to see difficult things as only bad, but if you can train yourself to think differently, you can gain a new view of the world.

Progress doesn't travel in a straight line and often it stalls because one way of thinking has taken us **as far as it can go.**

In these cases, a new way of thinking is required, and these new ways of thinking are often forced upon us by setbacks. Sometimes, the best way to fix a problem means looking at root causes that do not appear connected to it, like Toto Wolff did at Mercedes, whereas in other cases you will be required to find new ways, like Evelyn Glennie did with her music. Sometimes you need to adopt new perspectives, not just to overcome a problem, but to achieve a new, higher level of performance.

Take this example. If we asked you to cut a cake into eight equal pieces using only three cuts, could you do it? Have a think.

Like most people, you probably decided after some time that it was not possible. When you look down on a cake and make three slices, the most you can create is six equal pieces. But what if we looked at the cake from a new perspective? From above, and then horizontally, from the side.

If you cut the cake from above into four quarters with two cuts and then sliced through the cake horizontally (turning the four slices into eight) you would have achieved our goal. You would have done something that seemed impossible because you looked at your task from a new angle. If you approach problems from new directions, often you can then see them completely differently, and new solutions become available.

COMFORT ZONES

Approaching goals from new directions will also often mean trying new approaches, and this might require you to leave your comfort zone. This is potentially daunting, but you have to be conscious of how necessary it is for progress.

All progress is achieved at the edge of your comfort zone.

This is because you only feel comfortable when you know you can do something comfortably, and usually that means you have done it before. It is only by doing new things that are not yet comfortable for you that you can extend your range of possibilities and raise your ceiling.

Sports science captures this fact. The only way to develop muscles is through progressive overload, gradually adding weight to keep pushing at a level that is on the edge of your comfort zone. But if you only lift weights that you're comfortable lifting easily, your muscles will never be forced to grow to the new challenge. Equally, if you want to run your first five kilometres, you might have to progress through the stages of a fast walk at the edge of your comfort zone to one kilometre at the edge of your new boundary, then you set a new upper limit and run further – and you keep doing that until you reach your goal of five kilometres. Only then do new achievements become open to you. The part of the journey towards running five kilometres that is comfortable is before you start, when you're on the couch, and that is the one stage you must avoid staying at if you are to reach your goal.

Being comfortable also *becomes uncomfortable*. When you have no goals to reach for, or efforts that stretch you, it is natural to become bored, listless, and frustrated at your lack of progress. Discomfort and growth go hand in hand, so in a sense you have to learn to be comfortable with being uncomfortable. Fortunately, this is something we can practise. Football manager Graham Potter encouraged his players to perform songs for one another in a theatre to get comfortable with discomfort, while rock climber Alex Honnold told us that he saw the discomfort of his challenges as driving his happiness and wellbeing in his daily life.

You have to learn to **appreciate** a challenge.

This is the theory of living at the edge of your comfort zone, but it is also the thinking behind the growth mindset. A person with a growth mindset *enjoys* being challenged, whereas a person with a fixed mindset just wants to be congratulated for being how they are. A fixed mindset is only useful for conserving what you have or staying the same, and at this point in your life you will have goals and aims that require you to grow.

So appreciate the challenges and the setbacks; they are teaching you resilience and forcing you to grow. When you face a problem that requires a new form of thinking, feel gratitude for the lessons that it is teaching you and the perspective it might help you to acquire. Your challenges are like a personal trainer, presenting you with the progressive overload that will help you grow. The more hurdles you face, the better you will get at clearing them, so actively seek challenges. They will prepare you for the obstacles that life throws your way without your choosing.

If you can do that, you will have the mindset of Billy Monger and be capable of reaching for your dreams in the wake of even the harshest setback. You will demonstrate the flexibility and durability of Evelyn Glennie and be able to find new routes to progress even when all the old knowledge suggests your path has been blocked. You will have the resilience of Siya Kolisi and be ready to appreciate your hardships for what they are – experiences that make you tougher than you would be without them. These champions shared their lessons so that you can live by them. They flourished, so you can too.

KEY TAKEAWAYS

1. Break the cycle of pessimism when you experience small setbacks.

2. Feel in control by acknowledging negative thought patterns and changing them to more realistic ones.

    A. The pervasive: 'Everything is wrong' becomes 'This went wrong.'

    B. The permanent: 'I never succeed' becomes 'I didn't succeed this time.'

    C. The personal: 'I am an idiot' becomes 'How can I do better?'

3. Own your mistakes. Everyone makes them but high performers learn from them.

4. Accept setbacks and remember all that you can control is your response.

5. Life + Response = Outcome.

6. Think about the good things your setbacks can teach you.

7. Be prepared to pivot when you face a problem. Try to see things differently.

8. Step outside your comfort zone. This is where growth happens.

6

ACHIEVING GOALS

A GOAL IS not a single thing. It can be focused on changing the world or on changing yourself. It can have an end point, or it can centre on how you want to always be and therefore exist indefinitely. We've spoken to Olympic champion diver Tom Daley who sets himself three goals every day, and others like Dame Laura Kenny who had the goal of winning gold medals. There is room for all kinds of goals in the broad scope of high performance, but some have more impact, last longer, and feed into how you act all the time. These goals are usually intrinsic; they are about how you *feel inside.* They are about how you want to be, and therefore you can do them every day. They are powerful because any external or performance-related goal will be served by adopting these internal goals. We will discuss these **GOALS OF BEING** in more detail towards the end of the chapter but first, here is an example to plant the seed in your mind while we are discussing our approach to other types of goals.

If we offered you the magic power to achieve one of these two goals instantly, which would you choose?

I WANT MY DREAM JOB.

I WANT TO ALWAYS DO MY BEST.

What you might not realize is that the second goal *contains* the first. The second goal rises above the first because if you aim to always do your best, and you decide the one result of that is to be a lawyer, then it can be so. You will also have the freedom, after you have achieved the first goal, to pursue the goal of being the best lawyer you can be. Afterwards you can retire and pursue the goal of being the best gardener you can be. The second goal is preferable because, if your goal was only ever to become a lawyer, then you could achieve it and... what next? You'd have to start again, and this time you would probably decide that your goal will be to do your best, at whatever you choose next.

However, this is not to say that you shouldn't set yourself goals with end points. The power of a target is an incredible thing.

- A target can drive you to work hard.
- A target helps you to achieve focus and block out the things that may distract you.
- A target gives you something to celebrate.
- A target doesn't have to be an end in itself.

These goals, though, are really just results of *being* a certain way – they are a means to evaluate how you are working and behaving in terms of your non-negotiables and habits. Targets are a way to measure how your behaviours are working for you, but when you treat your goals as ends in themselves, you will likely face the challenge of what to do next.

The first thing you should do when you reach a target is, of course, celebrate. You should look back on the milestone and see how the small things you have done consistently can be packaged up into this achievement. You should rest for as long as you feel you need to and enjoy the company of people who understand how hard you have worked, but try to remember this:

The hard work in itself was the achievement.

The exam grade on the piece of paper is not the success, it is the way you applied yourself and the things you learned to achieve it. Think of it like this:

WOULD I RATHER A COMPUTER ERROR GAVE ME TOP MARKS IN ALL MY EXAMS BUT I LEARNED NOTHING, OR KNOW EVERYTHING AND RECEIVE A FAIL?

In the first example you have nothing but the paper that says you did well, but in the latter example you know that you have the habits, the knowledge, and the experience that really matter. If someone got top marks without doing the work, they would probably struggle at the next hurdle, whereas the person who received a fail would do their retakes, succeed, and go on to the next challenge, aware of their resilience and with the knowledge that was not recognized the first time.

Treat a celebration of a milestone as just that: a celebration, a moment in the present when you can enjoy your achievement. Do not let that distract you from the fact that there was a lot to enjoy about working towards it. The journey is always more important than the destination. In fact, you're better placed if you avoid thinking of your goals purely as destinations. The idea of a destination makes you think of a goal as an ending, when it is also a beginning and a middle. It is part of a journey, and learning to enjoy the journey is a goal in its own right.

Someone once said of the ancient empire-building King of Macedonia Alexander the Great (talk about a high performer – the man got 'the Great' added to his name!): 'And when Alexander saw the breadth of his domain, he wept for there were no more worlds to conquer.' Why do you think he wept? Was he *too great*? Was there just not enough conquering to do? Or did he choose a form of external motivation that had to run out at some point? We need to set goals to chart our progress, but not to finish our story, because that will lead us to weep, just like Alexander.

There is a similar phenomenon that people who commit to running a marathon often experience, known as 'post-marathon blues'. It happens when they set a target of running this distance and give everything to succeed. When they do, they often report feeling less motivated, happy, and purposeful than when they were yet to achieve it. It is almost as if the goal of running a marathon was a good thing until they reached it, but became a problem once it was achieved. The only antidote to post-marathon blues is to realize that it was not the goal nor the potential to achieve it that made them happy, but what they were doing. Pursuing the marathon made them happy, dedicating themselves to their fitness made them happy, and feeling proud of their dedication and drive did, too. Once marathon runners see that it is the continuous state of dedication that makes them feel satisfied rather than the acknowledgement at the end of it, they can learn something wonderful.

Happiness is not something that you can only experience in the achievement of a goal. It is something you can have all the time if you enjoy the things involved in pursuing it.

CREATING NEW GOALS FROM COMPLETED ONES

As Nietzsche pointed out, you don't climb a mountain to be on top of a mountain. You do it to *climb* a mountain, and once you have reached the peak, you have to find another one that you enjoy climbing. This is important in terms of your short-term goals. It is often helpful to think about new goals that branch off from your goals in the short term. Say, for example, you want to get a Grade 9 in your Spanish A level. You get it. The next move is to think about what you can do with that 9: a new goal that branches off from your previous one. Maybe you want to read a piece of Latin American literature in the original Spanish, or visit the Spanish city of Seville. Perhaps you want to climb to the ancient Inca city of Machu Picchu, high in the Andes Mountains of Peru. Another mountain has, in more ways than one, presented itself to you.

You can also take the achievement of a short-term goal and ask yourself, 'How can I use this to help people?' Perhaps your goal was to learn how to design a website. You achieved it. Now what? You could teach other people how to do it, too. That would allow you to grow as a person and a designer, as teaching has been shown to be one of the most effective learning tools out there. Or you could offer to improve the website of a local charity. This might satisfy another goal of being a helpful member of society, or of making a contribution. You could think of any number of ways in which the realization of your goal could have positive and powerful knock-on effects and save yourself from post-marathon blues – as long as you think of your goal as a beginning and not an end.

Think about the goals you have set for the near future.

HOW CAN THESE GOALS BE USED TO HELP OTHER PEOPLE?

WHAT NEW GOALS COULD BRANCH OFF FROM THEM?

It could be that you decide to use your recently achieved goal as a springboard for a new and bigger one. This would allow you to build from your achievements, but also to take stock of the processes and approaches you used previously and employ them again, only better. It would be a mistake not to do that, just as it would be a mistake to think that you only practised running every day to achieve a marathon, when actually you did it to improve your fitness and you enjoy running. If you limit all those improvements to the pursuit of one single goal, you close yourself off from the opportunities to put your skills to good use.

So you can take short-term goals and use them as springboards to work towards bigger and greater things, but there is also another component to effective goal setting that you should consider.

BIG HAIRY AUDACIOUS GOALS (BHAG)

Apologies for the big hair, but that is just how these goals come! In the words of James Collins and Jerry Porras, your BHAG is 'an audacious 10-to-30-year goal to progress towards an envisioned future'. It should be memorable, attention-grabbing, and *so big* that you and the people who support you can't help but be inspired. Think Google's mission to organize the world's information and make it accessible to everyone, and Greta Thunberg's mission to address climate change, and to inspire the world to work together for a sustainable climate and society, the ultimate goal being to save the planet.

- A Big Hairy Audacious Goal is one that exists at the **edge of imagination**. It stretches the idea of possibility and increases our sense of what is possible.

- A BHAG **raises your ceiling**; it creates a mountain climb that has a peak shrouded in mist, which is so attractive because it will mean going into the unknown.

It also helps that such a big goal allows you to see your short-term goals as mere stepping stones. Learning web design is one step towards the BHAG; teaching web design in a community group another. Creating a website that changes the world is a BHAG. The beauty is that you may not know *exactly* what the goals are in between your short-term aims and your BHAG, but you'll recognize them when you see them. You will not have to stand on top of the mountain of achievement and look back; you will use that mountain as a vantage point to seek out the next highest peak – the one that might let you see above the clouds of what is currently possible.

This may seem like a lot to take in from where you are right now. Your teenage years and the last few years of school are a time of freedom and limitation. People still tell you what to do, where to go, and what your achievements can be. You can do as well as you can, within the structure of education, but often not much better. However, once you're outside formal education structures, there is *no limit*. There is no Grade 9 at which you could not score any higher and there is no examination that marks the end of your progress. You will no longer have the structure of someone telling you what is right and wrong, but you will have the freedom to decide just how right you can be. It can be daunting, but it is also the greatest freedom you could ever have. This is where a BHAG focuses your mind on the new heights you can reach, rather than the safety nets you have to leave behind. You can decide on the upper end of your ambition for yourself, and if it sounds ridiculous then… so much the better. This is just what you're trying to do.

Maybe you decide you're going to be the greatest fashion designer that ever lived. No one can doubt what your ambition is. You have decided on that, but you have also committed to working to achieve this. You will have to focus in the way 'the greatest designer that ever lived' focuses, work as hard as the greatest would, and trust your instincts because you're going to be the greatest. Your BHAG offers a way of working back towards 'non-negotiables' from a future achievement; it is a way of ensuring that you graft like the person you're going to become. It is a Zander letter from the greatest fashion designer that ever lived. Compare the results of this BHAG to a more modest goal: 'I want to be a fashion designer'. How far does that goal push you forward? It pushes you as far as sewing some clothes. If you have designed a piece of clothing and made it, you're in some way a fashion designer, but now you need another goal to level that up. In doing so, you're being pushed upwards from your current position to new achievements, whereas a BHAG can pull you upwards to dizzy heights.

We should emphasize, though, that a BHAG alone is not enough. It is the 30-year plan that gives you faith in what you have to do today. A BHAG stands alone, but it is made up of single days and efforts.

A Big Hairy Audacious Goal
is the **result** of all the **smaller goals**
that went before it.

In the military, there is the concept of the **COMMANDER'S INTENT**. It is incredibly simple, and the perfect short-term companion to the complex and incredibly long-term BHAG.

Your commander's intent.

The commander's intent involves only two statements.

The objective tomorrow is to...

The single most important thing I can achieve is...

Try it now. What is your commander's intent for tomorrow?

Each evening you can create your own commander's intent, so that you can achieve your daily objectives and, in time, the days become weeks, years, and decades – they grow big and, erm, hairy... and turn into Big Hairy Audacious Goals.

In theory it is straightforward, but in practice, each day will provide you with new questions and challenges. You will have to learn to prioritize the path that leads to your big goal and leave behind those that take you away from it. You will have to learn to reject the things you don't need. If your BHAG is a mountaintop, you can't justify carrying extra weight.

CUT OUT WHAT YOU DON'T NEED

Many high performers engage in an exercise to help them think about what they *really want*. The key is to think about what you would do if money wasn't a factor and time was short. Psychologists often ask this question to prompt their clients to think about what is important to them: **IF YOU INHERITED £20 MILLION BUT WERE TOLD YOU HAD ONLY 10 YEARS TO LIVE, WHAT WOULD YOU DO?**

Your first inclination might be to say, 'I'd buy a mansion and spend my days on the beach.' OK – think about that a bit more deeply. Almost *every* high performer we interviewed had the means to buy a mansion and spend their days on a beach. Not one of them has chosen to live like that. There is meaning and purpose that they seek that a mansion and a beach simply cannot provide. A mansion is just a big house. Beaches feel special because we visit them on holiday. They will not feel quite so special if you're on a 10-year holiday before your death.

You will still want to achieve something. So what is it? And how can you achieve it in the short time span you have? Now your BHAG is down to a 10-year plan, how can you mark out the steps to reach your goal? You have to find what you are good at and what gives you meaning, then commit to it and all the effort that is required. You'll also need to find people who will help you achieve this goal in the short time you have.

So be aware of the things that *seem* important but only delay your progress. Don't forget you only have 10 years.

Create your own To Don't list.

Write down all the things that take up your time but get in the way of you achieving your goals in the 10 years.

What do you do just to 'pass the time'?

What could you be doing instead?

Anything you do to 'pass the time' will seem *very* different when your time is limited. Time will not be for passing; it will be for using, so ask yourself which of your habits or hobbies you really enjoy enough to justify doing them at the expense of the things that will help you to achieve your goals. Some enjoyable things will obviously pass the test and stay in your To Do list. Time with family and friends, or moments appreciating the beauty of the world are clearly time well spent, so they stay. But things that you know, deep down, you do just to pass the time have got to go. Playing games on your phone – got to go. They're a distraction and time is limited. Scrolling mindlessly on TikTok. Sorry, gone. However, that doesn't mean social media is completely off the table. Social media is an important entertainment and information network: many high performers and businesses understand how valuable it is to help them achieve their goals. If you're using social media to achieve your goals, to research, to broadcast, or to publicize, fantastic – but if you're *simply scrolling, then it is using you*. So get it on the To Don't list. These can also be considered non-negotiable because they are things you won't do in order to maximize your potential.

It is a strange fact that understanding what you *should* do often requires you to focus on what you *shouldn't* do. The To Don't list frees up time and mental space to think about what you want to achieve. This is important because many of us move through life on a form of auto-pilot, taking the opportunities that are offered to us and remaining in unsatisfying situations because we think we lack the time and space to imagine something better. Football manager Eddie Howe told us that when he left his successful stint as Bournemouth manager, he took a year to decide whether he wanted to continue coaching; he *didn't coach* in order to remind himself of *why he coached*. When he did return to a job at Newcastle, he knew why he was doing it, and felt motivated and confident in his decision. His story is a powerful reminder that pausing productively is more effective than driving forward aimlessly. The To Don't list can free up time for us to pursue our goals or to stop and consider them, but the key is to gain focus by removing distractions and then use that focus to move forward, mindfully.

Your life and the time you have are precious. How you spend your time should feel meaningful because your life is. So don't think of your time as something to pass, or to get through before the next experience. Use it.

If you can, find a way to be productive, and work towards your audacious goals with the support of other people. We can all find meaning and motivation in teamwork, and big goals always have a moment when a second pair of eyes helps us to see new paths, so find people who motivate you to be better. Create a culture that takes you towards your big goal with other people who share it.

Most of all:

Remember why you want to achieve your goal.

This takes us back to the start, to knowing ourselves. School and education give you reasons for working: your goals are set and other people are involved in managing your motivation. There will come a time when school is no longer the reason you work. No one will tell you what to do or why you should do it. It will be your choice, and you should choose something that motivates you, something that gives you an immediate answer to the question of 'Why am I doing this?' It's daunting, but all this freedom is liberating. So you have to know yourself and your purpose because that purpose will be what drives your commitment.

Football manager Sir Alex Ferguson often told his players this story to sum up his attitude to motivation. Three people were laying bricks, when a passer-by stopped and asked what they were doing. The first replied, 'Laying bricks.' The second said, 'Earning £10 an hour.' The third replied, 'I'm building a cathedral, and one day, I'll bring my children here and tell them that their dad contributed to this magnificent building.' The first labourer knew what they were doing, but didn't know why. The second knew why they were doing it, but the motivation was external. The third, however, completely understood why they were doing it. They had a BHAG to build a cathedral and that goal would take them through until the last tile was laid. The third labourer believed that they could build something greater than themselves, but they still wanted to do it *for their own achievement*. The joy of building a cathedral is far greater than that of laying bricks.

Every brick is a part of a cathedral when you have a BHAG. A Google software engineer is not just working; they are connecting the world. If we can imagine the big things, the smallest things shine with their purpose. And so do you.

Remember, though, that your purpose must be your own. If that third labourer had only wanted to build the cathedral to please a king, they would always be at the mercy of what the king wanted. On the final day, the king might decide he didn't like the structure and everything would have been in vain; whereas if the labourer loved building cathedrals, then they would not be disappointed, regardless of the king's opinion.

So maintain your internal locus of evaluation. If you're the final judge of your achievements, no criticism can derail you. No praise can distract you or make you big-headed. You will be your own driver and you will provide your own fuel. You can choose your car, your race, and the location of your finish line. You will be free, bound only by your own standards. This is empowering, but you must always remember *why* you are choosing to work hard.

IMPOSTOR SYNDROME

When you have clear goals and an understanding of why you pursue them, you have clarity and motivation, but you still have to take steps to remain positive and value your achievements along the way. Even when you succeed, you can doubt whether you really deserved to succeed. For many people this can form a pattern that is known as **IMPOSTOR SYNDROME**. It is common and something to be aware of, but it is also something you can take steps to manage and overcome.

Impostor syndrome is the experience of doubting your abilities and accomplishments compared with others, even when all the evidence from your experience suggests the opposite.

If you doubt whether you really deserve to achieve something, or believe that other people are wrong when they speak highly of your abilities, you're practising impostor syndrome. Many successful people have to learn to manage impostor syndrome and the fear that they may be exposed as a fraud. They have to remind themselves that their success is not just a matter of luck, but that they deserve the good things that come their way.

Entrepreneur Sara Davies told us that she'd experienced impostor syndrome during her first year as a *Dragon's Den* investor, but she came to understand that she had been chosen because others believed she was the best person. She wasn't there because she was lucky; she became a Dragon because she deserved the role. To paraphrase her advice: you just need to live up to the positive expectations that others have of you, be the best version of yourself and really own that.

It is important to take time to consider how you speak about yourself, *to yourself*, because impostor syndrome is basically about how you explain the world and your success to yourself. For example, you may consistently tell yourself that the bad things in your life are deserved, but the good things are lucky. This is inconsistent, and a form of pessimism that limits your achievements, but also your general happiness. Where possible, you should try to remember this:

The bad things in your life are either misfortune (over which you have no control) or mistakes (which we can learn from).

The good things are the results of your choices.

You should look back on your achievements and use them as an argument against the thought that you're an impostor. Focus on the consistent, small habits that make up the basis of your achievements. Finally, try to speak to people you trust when you have feelings of impostor syndrome. Share your doubts with them; they will likely be able to look at them from a different perspective.

All these things will help you to improve your **EXPLANATORY STYLE**. This follows the theory that you see the world, and yourself, positively or negatively – because of how you *explain* it. If you describe the things you achieve in terms of the hard work you do, then you will have a positive explanatory style. This builds a sense of control. You have control over the good things that happen in your life, and you have room to understand that you're not always responsible for the hardships. If you tend to blame yourself when bad things happen, or imagine that they will keep happening, you're trending towards a negative explanatory style. As much as possible, you should try to develop a positive explanatory style and a positive sense of control over your life for these reasons:

Positive events are permanent, universal, and internal.

Negative events are temporary, specific, and external.

Any achievement in your life should be noted and seen as a reflection of the good work you have done; any problem is a misfortune to be accepted and left behind, or a mistake to be learned from. The more effort you put into thinking this way, the more optimistic you will become, and you will have a better life outcome as a result. Your health, your working life, and your relationships will all improve if you can learn to feel optimistic and in control, so it is worth practising.

GOALS OF BEING

We have described Big Hairy Audacious Goals and we have described smaller goals that flow from one to another, to eventually become great things, but there is a thread that ties both of these types of goals together. High performance is focused on being the best you can be. This means knowing yourself well enough to realize what *your best* means to you and adopting approaches that help you to get there. But underneath it all there is one consistent theme: the importance of being.

The big idea of high performance is making the small things count, and the biggest thing is in fact the smallest one: how you are *being* in every moment. If this sounds philosophical or spiritual, then you're right – it is. Many philosophical and spiritual traditions have focused on how being present in the moment is key to a life well lived. They prioritize self-knowledge, who you want to be, and a dedication to proudly being that person in every second of every day. The power of setting the goal of *being* who you want to be, and *behaving* as that person would in each moment, is the foundation of every other goal and practice we have described.

Think of it like this. You may have focused goals and ways of judging your performance against them, but what happens if your underlying goals begin with the word 'being'? Being consistent. Being driven. Being optimistic. Being grateful. All your other goals will cascade from these underlying ones like a waterfall, and the practices of high performance will, too.

Being consistent leads you to the practice of:

Having non-negotiable habits.

Creating action triggers and trademark behaviours.

Being driven means:

Improving on your weaknesses.

Having an internal locus of control.

Being optimistic means:

Asking, 'How am I clever?'

Giving yourself positive labels.

Using your blue brain over your red brain.

Being grateful means:

Treating pressure as a privilege.

Seeing choices as freedom.

Writing gratitude lists.

All these practices come out of ways of being, and if you can focus on being these things, what you do and what you achieve follows naturally from them. These are the definition of internal motivations and they do not have an end point. No matter what you achieve, if you're being positive and being driven, you will have no problem finding the next goal. Having goals of 'being' solves the challenge of deciding on long-term goals, because the way you are creates new ones. You do not have to think about motivation or struggle to find it, because your way of being is motivated.

If you can focus on who you are, then your performance and your achievements will follow. You can possess a lifetime goal if you decide how you want to be, and then work on being that way, as much as you can. You can be grateful, driven, or optimistic anywhere, at any time, and in any discipline. You can be focused on being and, as a result, focus on the journey, rather than the destination. You can reach any mountaintop and feel exactly the same way standing there as you will feel at the bottom of the next mountain.

> However it is, you **choose** to be.

How do you want to be? If you could behave in certain ways for the rest of your life, what would those ways be? Would you be kind? Optimistic? Driven? Thoughtful? You can choose as many as you like.

WHAT IS MY BIG HAIRY AUDACIOUS GOAL?

WHAT WILL THAT REQUIRE OF ME?

HOW WILL I HAVE TO BE?

KEY TAKEAWAYS

1. Remember that achieving a goal isn't an end point. Learn to love pursuing it.
2. Think about how your small goals can branch off into new ones.
3. Look at how you can use what you have learned in pursuing your goal.
4. Create a Big Hairy Audacious Goal (10–30-year plan).
5. Use the commander's intent: What is my single main objective tomorrow?
6. Cut out the things you don't need. Create a To Don't list.
7. Focus on the why when you're pursuing a goal. The how will follow.
8. Fight impostor syndrome with a positive explanatory style. Achievements are the result of hard work; disappointments are misfortunes to forget or mistakes to learn from.
9. Think about how you want to be. Every day.

7 LOOKING WITHIN

ONE DAY, LONG before his 100-metre Olympic gold-medal win, Usain Bolt was a young boy running in primary school athletics competitions. He was not a champion or an inspiration; he was not the runner millions of people would cheer across a finish line. And yet, in another way, he was.

At the age of 15, to help her mum pay the bills, Susie Ma made a body scrub, using a recipe that her grandmother and mother had taught her. She filled 50 jam jars, took them to Greenwich Market – and sold them all on her first day. But that wasn't always the case. There were days when she made no money, her jars leaked, and her customers were unhappy.

These heroes did not become high performers the moment they crossed finish lines, or sold their first product. This happened long before world championships and business deals, and the hard work and hard times. They became high performers from the day they *committed* to their journeys and stuck to that commitment. Whether they were standing in running shorts or school uniform, Usain and Susie were once young people who looked forward and upwards, and who made the decision to climb. No one told them that they were a world champion in waiting or would one day be selling millions of their own products all over the world. No one marked out their paths for them. They chose to be their best, to study and train, to endure and believe, and to go from where they were in that moment to reach the greatest heights that they could.

For Usain, this meant renewing his commitment to high performance after his failure to compete in the 2004 Athens Olympics, when he didn't make it through the first round. In Susie Ma's case, she went on to become an investment banker, but she never gave up on her 'side hustle' as she worked on her skincare business during weekends and evenings. She felt that it was important to have options in life, but she came to realize that being an investment banker with lots of money was not the thing that would bring her happiness. So, she chose to step away from that career and instead returned to the path that enabled her to follow her passion.

From the start, they both committed to performing at a high level, and every time their mindset took them on to a new challenge, they approached it with the same purpose and intent. The journey was unmapped, but the approach was clear from day one.

START AT THE BEGINNING

Where are you at this moment? The likelihood is that you are in the very place where Usain and Susie once were. You are at the beginning, and it is an incredible place to be. The beginning deserves as much credit as the end. The start is equal to the finish in any journey, so stop and look around. You may be in a classroom or library, or in your bedroom or sprawled on the living-room floor, but you're surrounded by high performers. Every person who has ever maximized their potential is around you. Think of them as pictures on the wall. Dame Jessica Ennis-Hill was where you are now when she began her journey to Olympic golds. Siya Kolisi was once a young man who possessed hope and determination, just like you. Jo Malone was not born a millionaire, but the aspects of her personality and outlook helped her to become one. The ingredients of your success are within you; your journey towards it is yours only, but the high performers can be your guides.

This book can help to take you on the journey that all our high performers have taken. Your beginning is the same; your destination may differ, but the lessons they learned along their journeys are here to take you forward on yours. They are case studies that offer not directions but approaches.

They tell you to bring plenty of water, wear sturdy shoes, and plan the next part of your route when you reach a good vantage point. They do not tell you where you should go, but offer examples of *how* you should go. This will prove invaluable.

GET TO KNOW YOURSELF

The high performers we interviewed all had a common aspect in their lives: they started by getting to know themselves. This began on the day you were born, but you may have only made a *conscious* decision to do it recently. You made a choice to read this book. By doing so, you've started the journey to knowing yourself. It is only by knowing yourself that you can know what you want to achieve and who you want to be.

The part of your mind that you go to when you want to understand yourself is the place where all the journeys of high performers take shape, and one that you can return to whenever you need to change your route or approach. You may go on many journeys towards great achievements in your life, but you only need to learn the *value* of self-knowledge once. If you can learn *how* to see yourself, to listen to yourself, and appreciate yourself, then you are on the journey to high performance, and that journey could take you anywhere.

So take the time to reflect on these questions:

WHAT AM I MOTIVATED BY?

WHAT DO I ENJOY?

WHAT COULD I DEDICATE MYSELF TO?

You don't have to have just one answer to these questions. You can have as many as you like! Just like the high-performance journey in general, knowing yourself is not something that you do once; it is lifelong and it should be consistent. We all want to *be* someone who knows themselves and, for all that remains constant in you, you will change and you must stay aware of the ways in which you do. The great thing is that your goals can shift and grow with you; your goals can be as fresh at 80 years old as they are at 18. We are all beginners, in some way, all the time, and that is a wonderful thing. So be prepared to set new goals throughout your life, but stay consistent in who you are. The greatest goals are *to be* a certain way and they will underpin all your aims and targets. However, these goals may change during your lifetime. To be resilient, to know yourself, and to be grateful – these are goals that can take you towards any target of your choice, so you should always practise them and see how they lead you towards your targets.

Knowing yourself will mean understanding your strengths and your weaknesses, being grateful for the way in which you are clever, and turning that gratitude into responsibility. *You* have been given something, and only you can decide how you use it to give back. If you can understand your skills, and be grateful enough to share them with the world, then all that remains is to think about how you can use your skills in a way that gives you meaning. If you can discover something that challenges you while building on your strengths and that offers you flow states, then your motivation will become a renewable resource. When you know what you *love doing*, the act of doing it will motivate you. So discover how you are clever, apply it in a way that you love, and your work will never feel like work at all.

Keep thinking about *who* you want to be, and *how* you want to be. This is both a goal and a way of thinking about your non-negotiables and your trademark behaviours. The things you do each and every day become who you are. So decide on how you want to be and commit to the small, simple behaviours that will together make up your identity.

These commitments will help you achieve higher performance, but they will also help you in moments when you have to make a choice. If you have decided to *be someone committed*, that small choice to get up early and train will no longer be a choice; it will be a trademark behaviour. If you have decided to be a flexible thinker, then you will be able to make choices and approach problems in ways that other people may miss.

MAINTAIN YOUR IDENTITY

Find strength in your non-negotiables and who or how you have decided to be, because that will also give you a thread of consistency when plans change. If you miss a goal, who you are will not change, although your plans may do. You can be just as diligent the day after a disappointment as you were the day before it, and your identity will not be impacted by it. This gives you the freedom to change plans, to switch goals, and to find newer, more rewarding paths.

You are not your achievements and you are not your failures.

A failure to achieve a goal is not a failure in your identity. The only goals that concern your identity are how you would like *to be*, not what you would like to do or achieve. The victories and losses will come and go, but your state of being will be a constant.

Be consistent.

This consistency is what will mark you out and give you an advantage as the small things tally up. Call yourself a high performer. Say your goal is to always be diligent, creative, kind, or whatever it is that matters to you, and then let your actions follow. You can make a choice to create a positive label for yourself, and you can let that positive label guide your choices.

You have the freedom to choose.

Your goals, your path, your peer group, and your mentors. We all have to accept the fact that we choose the path of our lives, so make the choice to be an independent thinker and doer, who is comfortable standing out from the crowd if need be. You have to take responsibility for this choice, and see the value of standing out rather than someday regretting your decision to just fit in. This would be a mistake, and mistakes are better recognized and owned as soon as they are committed.

Be accountable and learn from your mistakes.

You will make mistakes, but they will teach you as much as your successes. But don't fear them. We all make mistakes, and the only true mistakes we could make are if we pretend they haven't happened, by refusing to take responsibility for them or failing to learn from them. Once you accept that you have made a mistake, you can free yourself from regret (mistakes that you didn't learn from) and from anxiety (the fear of making a mistake). You can step into pressurized situations and know that you have understood your skills, made the choice to build on them, and prepared yourself to learn from your mistakes.

Be aware of your feelings.

Recognizing your emotions will help let your blue brain take charge of your red brain. You have made the decision to be self-aware and in control, and now you have the techniques to make sure you are, even when the pressure is on. When you feel the pressure rising and instincts like fear or anxiety are taking over, you know how to stop, be aware of your emotions and what's happening, and find a better way to approach the situation. If you have learned to prepare, and remembered how to manage your red brain in pressurized situations, then there is no challenge that you cannot take on. Mistakes may be made, but you will have done everything correctly and there will be no room for regrets.

When a hurdle appears in your path, whether it is misfortune or a mistake, you will know that you can clear it or learn how better to clear the next one. You will discover just how good you are at picking yourself up and carrying on or starting again.

You're in control – your life is yours and your success is in your hands.

This is a form of pressure, but it's also freedom, so focus on growing, improving, and progressing. As you step out on your journey from the beginning, you will see that there is no end – only progress. There are no failures, only challenges, and there are no setbacks, only new opportunities.

STEP FROM COMFORT TO COURAGE

The greatest step we ever take out of our comfort zone is from childhood to adulthood, and that step, which you're taking now, brings both challenge and reward. Just as you would not want to stay a child forever, you would not want to remain in the other zones that have grown comfortable either. If you want to be smarter, faster, or stronger, then you must seek experiences at the edge of what you think is possible, because that is the way you will grow. Soon, what seemed uncomfortable will become comfortable too, then you will move on and grow again.

So what now? You know what it takes to achieve high performance. You are getting to know yourself. You know you can make choices, clear hurdles, and achieve your goals. Are you ready?

If you don't feel ready, then ask yourself:

WHAT IS THERE TO FEAR?

AM I AFRAID TO TRY MY BEST?

AM I WORRIED THAT I WON'T BE GOOD ENOUGH?

If you answer yes to the last two questions, don't worry – you're not alone! Every high performer has felt fear and experienced doubt, even when they are at the top of their game. The key is that they also learned about courage. Courage is not avoiding fear or hiding it. Courage is *feeling* your fear, *embracing* it, and finding a way to *thrive* because of it.

Professional boxer Josh Warrington told us that fear for him was like a fire; he could either use it as an energy source or get burned. As a boxer, he stepped into one of the most intimidating arenas in sport, and he learned that fear was not avoidable but necessary. He powered himself on fear, and he never got burned.

Ironically, the only way we are burned by our fear is when it freezes us and stops us from trying, when we want our fear to offer us a way out, or when we want to believe we are not enough because this is easier than trying to be great. So, ask yourself what a life lived in fear would actually be like. How would you look back on your life at the end knowing that you hadn't tried?

If you're feeling afraid of failure, ask yourself these questions:

HOW BAD WOULD IT BE IF I FAILED?

HOW WOULD I FEEL IF I FAILED AND HADN'T MADE ANY EFFORT TO AVOID IT?

HOW WOULD I FEEL IF I FAILED BUT I'D TRIED MY BEST?

Giving your all is not only the most satisfying route but also the least frightening. There is nothing to fear if you know you have done your best.

YOU ARE READY

Step forward from the beginning and start your journey. You are the author of your own story, the captain of your ship, and the master of your destiny. You can take your journey in any direction you choose; you can decide which rewards matter to you and the approaches that will help you achieve your goals. You are in control, and you will feel more in control as you move forward, applying the principles of high performance from this book.

You have already made it so far and you have many skills. The most powerful lessons come during difficult times, and they will test your grit, your endurance, and your determination. However, both good and bad events will contribute to your perspective of the world. Everyone faces challenges, but if you decide you're going to learn how to overcome them, then those skills can be added to what you already know, and you will be more prepared when the next challenge comes along. The approaches you adopt to prepare for your school exams will serve you in interviews – whether they are for university, a job, or an apprenticeship – and they will help you at university or wherever you choose to go after you leave school. What is true is that there will likely be many pressurized situations in your adult life, but you will have the skills to handle them.

The practice of getting to know yourself will not only be useful as you begin your journey into adult life, but at every significant juncture within it. Learning how to clear one hurdle will make you better at clearing the next. All your experiences, good and bad, are formative, if you treat them as life lessons.

Picture Usain Bolt as he started on his journey when he ran his first race in primary school, and Susie Ma as she set foot in Greenwich Market, ready to sell her home-made body scrubs. Think about everything they did not yet know. Think about all the high performers we've talked about in this book. Now think about their journeys so far. They tried and they failed. They worked hard and they learned. They practised and persevered. They *became* high performers, and they started out just like you. So go and join them.

QUICKFIRE QUESTIONS

We have arrived at the end, and of course we should treat it as a new beginning. As you progress on your high-performance journey, here are some questions that you can return to whenever you need to. Maybe you're facing a challenge that requires you to stop and think about yourself and your goals; you could have a choice to make or a hurdle to clear. Maybe you have suffered a disappointment. You know that these are moments that all high performers face, but they are challenges that help you grow and moments where you can learn, so use these questions to guide your thoughts. Your choices are your own, but the wisdom of high performance can help you to make the best choice for you.

You can answer these questions in your mind or on paper. You can run through all the questions if you're not sure how best to deal with your challenge, or you could focus on an individual question as a journal prompt. The key is to think about yourself, about what you're looking for, and to decide which thoughts and which practices will help you gain a sense of perspective and control over your situation.

KNOWING YOURSELF

What are your top three strengths?

List three moments when you have put them to use in the last year.

Describe some situations you might face in the next year where your strengths can be put to good use.

How are you clever?

Describe a goal or field of work where your type of intelligence can flourish.

Try to think of something that is outside your comfort zone or your normal expectations, where your type of intelligence could be applied in an interesting way.

What are your significant areas for improvement?

Have you already made efforts to improve on them?
What did you do?

If you haven't started yet, what are the small goals you could achieve in order to improve yourself?

What sort of challenges do you enjoy so much that you can become lost in them?

For these challenges, were the rewards internal or external?
If a reward was external, would you have done the challenge if you hadn't had this reward?

Have you ever done something hard purely because you enjoyed it?
What did it feel like when you were completing this challenge?

What kind of person do you want to be?

Describe five qualities in the form: 'I want to be...'
(for example, kind, hard-working, consistent).

Now apply these five qualities to goals you have.

MAKING CHOICES

What is your plan A?

What is your plan B if plan A can't happen?

What about your plans C and D?

What is something you need to do but struggle to find the motivation to do it?

How could you create an action trigger to do it?

Find something you always do and say, 'When I do that, I will [do the thing you struggle to do].'

What is a bad choice that you've made, that you need to understand and learn from?

Have you experienced a setback that was beyond your control? How did you react to it? How could you have responded better?

What is your preferred approach to dealing with anxiety?

HANDLING PRESSURE

What is the next pressurized situation you will face?

List the things that you already know that will help you to deal with it.

Visualize this pressurized situation in depth and detail.

Break it down into its components.

How do you prefer to deal with stress?

Talking? Planning? Exercising?

If you are unsure about your preference, then think of a stressful situation. How did you deal with it? Did you try one of these strategies: talking, planning, or exercise? How did it go? Think about the strategies you didn't apply. Would they have helped?

CLEARING HURDLES

What is the biggest hurdle you've cleared in the past year?

What did you do? How did it feel?

Is there a bad thing that 'always' happens to you? How can you think of this differently in a way that gives you a sense of control?

Is there a hard thing you cannot do but want to try? Add the word 'yet'.

Have you had the opportunity to 'pivot' when you faced a hurdle? How did you decide that you needed to pivot?

Choose a recent achievement, whether big or small – how could the lessons of that experience be applied to bigger challenges going forward?

ACHIEVING GOALS

What are your goals right now?

What are some new ones that could branch off from them?

How could your goals allow you to help people?

What could be your Big Hairy Audacious Goal?

How do you want to be? There is not just one answer here. You can think of lots of different ways you want to be!

ACTIVITIES

This is a recap of all the activities that came up in the book. Come to this section when you want to refresh your mind or your perspective.

KNOWING YOURSELF

1. Understanding your intelligence (or intelligences)

What is my intelligence (or intelligences)?

What do I find difficult at school?

How could my intelligence be applied to my challenge?

2. The possibilities of your types of intelligence

Think of your types of intelligence.

List a few careers that fit with these various types. (You could ask a careers guidance counsellor – if your school has one – for help if you're stuck for career ideas.)

Next, picture a friend or family member who has a different type of intelligence to you.

What could your intelligence plus theirs make?

Examples:

I have naturalistic intelligence; my sister is numerically intelligent. We could start an amazing landscaping business: I'll do the flowers and she'll do the accounts.

My mate has amazing linguistic intelligence, but I'm all about the interpersonal connections. She could be a writer, and I'll be her agent.

3. Positive labelling

Write down five things that you're good at and/or things you're proud you've done. If you're not sure, think about times when someone said you were good at something or praised something you've done.

Next to each one, write down the skills that made these achievements possible.

Keep coming back to this list, and think about how you're doing with them.

Are you improving in any of the skills?

Are you applying the same skills elsewhere?

Is there something you can do to improve a skill?

4. Your strengths and weaknesses

Write your strengths in one column.

Write your weaknesses in the other column.

Remember: these are more than just skills or talents.

Your strengths and weaknesses can be repeated behaviours, mindsets you have developed, or aspects of your personality.

Could one of your strengths help one of your weaknesses?

Draw a connecting line from one of your strengths to a weakness, to think about how the strength can help to improve the weakness.

You can try this exercise for different strengths and weaknesses, and also come back to it after a while. You might find that your strengths and weaknesses change over time.

5. Things you can and cannot control

Make a list of all the things that are outside your control in the build-up to your exams. (For example, late buses, or even a thunderstorm on the way to the exam hall.)

Next, list the things that are within your control. (For example, leaving early, packing waterproof gear... and revising.)

6. Your state of flow

Think of a time when you were totally focused on a task. When you did not have to 'think about thinking'; you simply acted.

Write it down and describe what you felt. (Many people describe the feeling as being like the flow of a river: their thoughts or actions connect without needing a push or a pull.)

7. Create a 'flow chart'

Draw a Venn diagram with three overlapping circles. One circle represents 'Things I find challenging'; another circle represents 'Tasks I enjoy'; and the third circle represents 'Tasks I do well'. Make sure there is room to write in the overlapping sections.

Fill each circle with tasks that are relevant to what the circle represents. Those that could fit into two or three circles should be in the parts that overlap. Those that fit into all three are activities for which you're more likely to access flow states.

8. Create your own Zander letter

Date it one year from now, and write it to yourself.

Begin with the words 'Dear [your name]'.

Then detail all the steps you took towards your goal.

It should not include any phrases such as 'I hope','I will', or 'I plan to'.

This is a letter from your future self, who has already achieved the goal, so it should all be in the past tense, and be absolute, 'I did' or 'I made'.

Include as much detail as possible: everything from the time of day you would usually wake up, to your meals and your work schedule.

Try to include some setbacks that you 'overcame'.

9. Create your trademark behaviours

Think about the positive labels you have for yourself.

What are the trademark behaviours you want to associate with these labels?

10. Create a ritual for an exam

List a set of behaviours that you will do every time you have a test (beyond revision, of course!). This set of behaviours will become your ritual.

The behaviours might include your wake-up time, your choice of breakfast, and the way you enter the exam hall.

Practise these behaviours on regular school days. For example, enter a classroom in the way that you might enter the exam hall.

This helps you feel in control, sets your standards, and reminds you that an exam is simply another routine.

It follows a process, and it is something you have done many times before.

MAKING CHOICES

1. Small choices you can make

Pick a big goal that you have.

Now make a list of the small choices that might make a difference while you pursue it.

2. Create your own daily routine

Devise a daily routine based on action triggers that work for you.

You can use the following as an example:

When I wake up, I will brush my teeth.

While I brush my teeth, I will look at my revision cards on the bathroom wall.

After I look at them, I will eat breakfast.

When I finish breakfast, I will lay out my revision materials.

After I lay out my materials, I will read through my textbook.

While I read through my textbook, I will make notes.

After I finish my notes, I will have lunch.

After lunch, I will turn my notes into revision cards.

And so on...

HANDLING PRESSURE

1. The power of visualization

Think of a challenge you will likely face in the next year.

Next, try to visualize yourself stepping into it.

Who is there? What kind of place are you in?

Finally, picture yourself doing exactly what you set out to do.

2. Break down a challenge

Pick a task you have to complete in the coming months. Maybe it is a test, an application, or a competition.

What are the parts that make up this challenge? Break it down into as many small parts as possible.

Is any one of these parts beyond your ability?

3. Your confidence bank account

Take a moment to catalogue your skills. Think about it like a confidence bank account that you can top up whenever you want – for free. This account will be a resource for when your red brain is taking over.

Ask yourself these questions:
What am I great at?
What skills do I have?
Most importantly, what is it that I simply know I can do?

4. Dealing with disappointment

Think of a time when you tried to achieve something and didn't succeed.

Picture how you would react to that situation with two different mindsets. One is an external focus, where most of your thoughts are about how other people perceive you, and the other is with your own internal locus of evaluation, where you were mostly judging your own effort.

What did you find when you judged your own effort? Did you think you could have done more – and could therefore learn something from it? Or did you think that you did your best and couldn't control the outcome? Both these observations are better than thinking about external judgement.

5. Affirmations

Write an affirmation. Something kind and supportive about yourself, such as 'I make an effort for my friends.'

6. Gratitude lists

Write a list of three things you're grateful for today.

CLEARING HURDLES

1. Yet...

Think of something that you'd like to achieve, but can't do. Now add the word 'yet'.

How are your feelings about this thing different now that you have applied the magic of a growth mindset?

2. Setbacks

Think about a setback in your own life.

What did you learn from it?

ACHIEVING GOALS

1. Branching goals

Think about the goals you have set for the near future.

How can these goals be used to help other people?

What new goals could branch off from them?

2. Your commander's intent

The objective tomorrow is to...

The single most important thing I can achieve is...

3. Your To Don't list

Write down all the things that take up your time but get in the way of you achieving your goals in the next 10 years.

What do you do just to 'pass the time'?

What could you be doing instead?

4. Your ways of being

How do you want to be? If you could behave in certain ways for the rest of your life, what would those ways be?

Would you be kind? Optimistic? Driven? Thoughtful? You can choose as many as you like.

5. Your Big Hairy Audacious Goal

What is your Big Hairy Audacious Goal?

What will that require of you?

How will you have to be?

YOUR HIGH PERFORMANCE TOOLKIT

These are some suggestions of phrases and thoughts that you could add to your High Performance Toolkit. Create a toolkit that works for you. Record inspiring quotes or statements that help you to maintain your focus.

Be **consistent**

Be **driven**

Be **grateful**

Be **optimistic**

Own your **mistakes**

You can't **control** misfortunes

Remember how you are **clever**

Choose **positive** labels

Have non-negotiable **habits**

Know your **strengths**

Know your **weaknesses**

Apply trademark **behaviours**

Pressure is a privilege

Think **flexibly**

An **end** is a new **beginning**

Life + Response = **Outcome**

GLOSSARY

action trigger – an action that you carry out that follows on from a previous action. Sticking to a series of action triggers can help you to form good habits and also means that you spend less time on planning what you need to do.

affirmation – a positive statement that you say to yourself. It should be kind and supportive, in order to challenge stress-provoking, negative thoughts.

autonomy – the ability to choose what you want to do, and to make your own well-considered decisions.

big choice – an important decision that you make for yourself that will have an impact on your future, and ideally a positive one. Thinking about and changing the sense of who you are or want to be, for the better, is a big choice that you can make for yourself.

Big Hairy Audacious Goal (BHAG) – an audacious 10-to-30-year goal to progress towards an envisioned future. It can be as ambitious as you like; the intention is to encourage you to stretch your goals, step by step – and you might just reach your BHAG.

capability – the ability to do something well, using the skills and resources that you have. Sometimes we need someone else to tell or remind us that we are capable of doing something, because we might not realize what we are good at.

catastrophizing – the tendency to focus on imaginary (and often negative or worst-case) consequences, but remember: energy spent on a hypothetical worst-case outcome could just as easily be spent thinking about a hypothetical best-case scenario.

celebrate – it's important to recognize an achievement and to enjoy the moment when a goal is reached. Your achievement is the result of all the small and big things you've done that led up to that moment.

commander's intent – two statements for the next day that set out your objective for the day and the one thing you want to achieve. Used correctly, the commander's intent can help you to prioritize the path that led to your big goal.

compartmentalizing – the act of breaking down a large challenge into smaller, more manageable tasks.

competence – the ability to do something well and to feel confident about it.

complement – when something or someone works well with another, and often the two (or more) together might lead to a stronger outcome. For example, if you work with someone whose strength is your weakness (such as maths), then their skills will complement yours, and you will likely become a stronger team.

confidence bank account – an internal catalogue of your skills, so you can remind yourself what you're good at, especially in moments of doubt.

conscious – to be actively mindful of your thoughts and feelings, and your strengths and weaknesses. To be conscious of these aspects of yourself is to be self-aware.

controlling the controllables – reminding yourself that you can't influence things that are beyond your control, but you can do your best to control your behaviour and how you respond to a situation.

courage – the strength to feel your fear, to embrace it, and to find a way to thrive because of it.

cycle of pessimism – where your negative thoughts about a situation will likely lead to poor performance, which then leads to more negative thoughts and poor outcomes, and this gets repeated. A cycle of pessimism turns one problem into a journey of disappointment.

dopamine reward system – the reward system in our brains that triggers the feeling of pleasure. It developed as a way for our brains to tell us that we had found something good or that we had achieved something difficult.

explanatory style – the way you explain the world to yourself, which affects how you see the world. If you have a positive explanatory style, you'll likely view challenges as opportunities or as only temporary. A person with a negative explanatory style will often see setbacks as permanent and think that bad things always happen to them.

flow state – the state of being so absorbed and focused on doing something that you lose track of time, your surroundings, and your worries. In a flow state, you often feel that you're in control.

foundation – the underlying, important values upon which something is built.

golden seed moment – an important moment when you realize that you can do or achieve something that you didn't think about before.

gratitude list – a list of things that you are grateful for. Writing a gratitude list can help to manage stress and pressure, and promote good mental health.

growth mindset – having the belief that you are the sort of person who can overcome challenges, and that you can grow and change.

habit – a behaviour that is repeated so often that it becomes automatic, often as part of a daily routine.

high performance – being able to consistently perform/act/work to the best of your abilities, often in a given area, but doing so needs focus, skill, and commitment.

implementation intention – another phrase for an action trigger; the intention to carry out an action.

intelligence – the ability to learn and apply knowledge and skills, but there is no one way to be intelligent. See page 23 for some of the ways that a person can be intelligent.

internal locus of evaluation – having an internal sense of who you are. It is not tied to the opinions of others, nor the results you achieve, but is instead your ability to evaluate your own effort based on your own standards.

intuition – the ability to know or do something instinctively, without having to spend time thinking about it first.

'know thyself' – an inscription upon the Temple of Apollo, from the time of the ancient Greeks. It's a simple but powerful instruction: if you want to understand the world, the best place to start is by understanding yourself, and that includes knowing your strengths and your weaknesses, your feelings, and motivations.

labelling – the act of creating an identity, or label, for yourself, which can help to shape how you think about yourself and how you behave.

marginal gains – the idea that small improvements can be combined to create a significant positive change.

mindset – a person's way of thinking, which can affect how they respond to challenges, opportunities, and situations.

misfortune – a setback, or unfortunate event, that is beyond your control.

mistake – an error that can happen as a result of misunderstanding or lack of knowledge, but it should be seen as something you can learn from.

motivation – the drive that pushes you to take action and work towards a goal. For high performance, it's better to be driven by internal motivation rather than be motivated by external rewards.

non-negotiables – things that you will always do (such as always getting up at the same time) because they connect who you are with what you want to achieve. They can also free up your mind to focus on more important decisions. Non-negotiable behaviours, when repeated consistently, create habits.

permanent thinking (or permanence) – when you treat a problem as if it will exist forever, which can lead to feelings of helplessness.

personal thinking – when you face a setback and think it is the result of a problem with yourself as an individual.

pervasive thinking – when you take a single problem and take it to mean that everything has gone or will go wrong.

pivot – to change from one goal to another, especially if you have not been able to achieve your initial goal. You can do this if you're able to think flexibly.

pursuit of self-knowledge – the process of using self-awareness to get to know yourself better. This ongoing development is at the heart of high performance; having a strong base (in other words, a strong sense of who you are) makes it easier for you to grow and achieve your goals.

relatedness – the idea of social support: being connected with others, especially when working together as a team.

resilience – the ability to accept that disappointing and sometimes terrible things are a part of life, and then being able to carry on with trying to achieve your goals.

ritual – a repeated sequence of behaviours, which can help to establish routine and maintain a sense of control.

self-awareness – to be actively mindful of your thoughts and feelings, and your strengths and weaknesses. If you are self-aware, you will be better at making the best decisions for yourself and at controlling your behaviour.

self-belief – being confident in your skills and capabilities, knowing that you have the capacity to learn and that you are able to be your own judge.

self-determination – the idea that you can control your own life and have an internal sense of motivation.

self-efficacy – the idea that you are in control of your future and you can make changes for yourself.

self-fulfilling prophecy – when you think negatively about yourself, and then behave in a way that leads to the negative outcome that you were worried about.

self-talk – how you speak to yourself, which can impact how you think about yourself and how you behave. Be kind and supportive to yourself in order to achieve the best outcome.

To Don't list – a list of things that you should avoid doing, in order to save your time and energy for more important goals.

trademark behaviours – behaviours and actions that are effectively non-negotiable, which are linked to the positive labels that you give yourself, for example, always having vegetables with every meal, or always holding the door open for the person immediately behind you.

visualizing – the practice of picturing yourself in a situation (often challenging or stressful) and thinking about the surroundings, your feelings, and what you are going to do. This allows you to engage in deeper, clearer planning, and also helps you to face the fear of the unknown.

yet – an important word that reminds you that you might not be able to do something in the present, but it's possible that you will in the future.

THE HIGH PERFORMANCE FOUNDATION

Too many young people lack the resilience they need to reach their full potential, and alarmingly up to one in five children also face significant mental health challenges.

The High Performance Foundation was created when hundreds of parents, teachers, and coaches who listened to 'The High Performance Podcast' messaged the team to say the learning was needed in schools. The charity is empowering young people to be able to write their own story and believe their capacity to achieve is found within, no matter their background.

Our vision is simple but ambitious:

Building young people's resilience and mental strength today so they can thrive tomorrow.

Our in-school programmes are transforming lives, teaching vital social and emotional skills, and providing young people with greater confidence, resilience, and wellbeing. We're empowering them to navigate the challenges they face, set meaningful goals for their future, and develop the key employability skills they need to succeed, equipping all young people with the tools to build resilience today, so they can thrive tomorrow.

HIGH PERFORMANCE FOUNDATION

THE HIGH PERFORMANCE PODCAST

www.youtube.com/@HighPerformancePodcast

WATCH ON YOUTUBE

The quotes in this book are from 'The High Performance Podcast' or *High Performance: Lessons from the Best on Becoming Your Best*, and we thank the contributors for allowing us to use their words. You can search our YouTube channel for the videos with individual interviews or check out the playlists for themed collections.

Authors Oscar Millar, Jake Humphrey, and Damian Hughes

Editors Francesca Harper, John Hort, Sophie Parkes
Additional Editorial Andrea Mills, Wendy Shakespeare
Art Editor Prateek Maurya
Project Art Editor Joe Lawrence
Jacket Designer Elle Ward
Managing Art Editors Anna Hall, Govind Mittal
Senior Production Controller Leanne Burke
Production Editor Dragana Puvacic
Art director Mabel Chan
Associate Publishing Director Francesca Young

Sensitivity Reader Lisa Davis
Proofreaders Petra Bryce, Polly Goodman

First published in Great Britain in 2026 by
Dorling Kindersley Limited
20 Vauxhall Bridge Road,
London SW1V 2SA

The authorised representative in the EEA is
Dorling Kindersley Verlag GmbH. Arnulfstr. 124,
80636 Munich, Germany

10 9 8 7 6 5 4 3 2 1
001–348904–Mar/2026

A CIP catalogue record for this book
is available from the British Library.
ISBN: 978-0-2417-3444-5

Printed and bound in Great Britain by Clays Ltd, Elcograf S.p.A.

www.dk.com

MIX
Paper | Supporting responsible forestry
FSC™ C018179
www.fsc.org

This book was made with Forest Stewardship Council™ certified paper – one small step in DK's commitment to a sustainable future.
Learn more at www.dk.com/uk/information/sustainability